A Myth For Our Time

A Myth For Our Time

Sir Bernard Burrows

Elizabeth Byron-Lindley

First published in 2001 by Elizabeth Byron-Lindley

British Library Cataloguing in Publication Data.
A Catalogue record for this book is available
from the British Library.

ISBN 0 95404 610 2

The jacket is based on a painting by Anne Norwich, 'Playing God'.
She has very kindly authorised its reproduction.

Typeset by CBS, Martlesham Heath, Ipswich, Suffolk

Printed and bound by Antony Rowe Ltd., Chippenham

Chapter 1

Myths

Why do we need a myth at all? There are two main kinds of reason for which people have invented myths. One is the general wish to believe in something beyond or superior to the physical world which surrounds us, something more powerful than ourselves which can help us to survive the changes and chances of our mortal life. In some ways the world was more dangerous for primitive men than it is today. They were more exposed to the elements and to the threats of other living creatures, both animals and humans. Disease and death came more frequently and earlier, and there were no antibiotics, so consequently there was a more easily perceived need for protection against these dangers. The protection seemed to come in early life from father or mother – first one then the other according to the theory that matriarchy preceded patriarchy. Therefore, goddesses and gods tended to be made in the image of the mother and father. Perhaps the very fact that life was considerably shorter added to the need for belief in a supernatural power. Men and women were alive on earth for such a comparatively short time that there was all the more need to have that time protected, and also to have some sort of a prolongation of life through mythical ideas of survival. Animals were both a danger and a necessity for food, hence the tendency of the shaman to identify himself with the animals both to ward off their anger and to assuage their spirits before taking their lives. Within living memory there has been in the Abruzzi region of central Italy an annual Festa dei Serpenti at which statues of the virgin and saints are paraded through the streets, festooned with living snakes, in the belief that this will make their worshippers less liable to be bitten during the coming year. Also, people were closer to the annual events of the natural cycle and particularly dependent on the rebirth in the spring, which seemed to hold out the prospect of existence being possible for a further year, and thus gave rise to myths of resurrection and fertility rites designed to make sure that the cycle continued. Certain places could easily be felt to be numinous, that is to say conducive to the idea of some supernatural presence, such as in the classical world the Lake of Nemi in central Italy, the site of the myth of the 'Golden Bough', and the source of the Adonis river in Lebanon where the water that is to form the river gushes out from an underground source, and which has been celebrated by religious buildings and rites during several civilisations.

These are some of the early incentives to myth-making, and modern parallels could quite easily be found among the few remaining primitive people in the world today, and possibly also among those who would consider themselves more sophisticated. Psychologically it is, no doubt, part of the unconscious urge to return to the safety and security of the womb, the wish to put responsibility for what happens, and for any decisions that are required, back onto somebody or something else. This has been a powerful element in the creation of religions. The general feeling of the numinous is usually broken down into the belief in a god, as being more like the human beings who have these feelings. In other words, as has often been said, we make gods in our own image, but without the limitations which are imposed on ourselves. We like to imagine gods as being freer than we are to take decisive action, and also as being more likely to continue in existence when we have departed this life. Sometimes, on the other hand, we push the similarity so far that we wish gods to be vulnerable or of finite life, just as we are ourselves.

The overthrow of the Titans by the Gods in Greek mythology might be one example. The death of Osiris, the death of Christ on the cross and the destruction of the whole Valhalla system in Götterdämmerung might be other examples. In some cases, this decline or disappearance of the gods is followed by resurrection. This is not exactly in the image of man as man, but responds to an innate wish of human beings that their death might not be the final extinction of their personalities. It may be noted, too, that in this category of myth-making the personages of the myth may be evil as well as good. The god of the underworld tended to be created at about the same time as the god of the earth or sky. The devil in the form of the serpent was the first thing that Adam and Eve met after the god who had created them. The devil had as much effect on the future as the original creator. For the Manicheans the principle of evil was as real as the principle of good, and they remained in eternal competition. Presumably this invention of a malevolent presence, as well as of a beneficent one, was due to the need to explain the unpleasant aspects of life, which everyone has experienced. Some people found it easier to think that the good and evil parts of experience were put there by two rival beings, rather than to think that a single being could alternately produce both aspects of life. In some oriental religions, the dichotomy is applied to the material and non-material aspects of our life. The material is equated with illusion and evil, and the spiritual with the good.

So these are some of the reasons for the imagination of gods – something bigger than ourselves to turn to for help in times of trouble or to ward off as the personification of evil.

The other reason for the creation of myths is to fill gaps in the description of the world as we see it and feel it by means of reason. This assumes that we start with a wish to apply reason as the explanation of what we see and what happens to us. So in our attempts to describe what we see, we build up a system of cause and effect. Nothing is supposed to happen without a cause that we can explain. But in the past, before our surroundings could be analysed, our ancestors frequently came upon things that they could not find a reasonable cause for. Therefore, the only way they were able to account for what happened was to invent some supernatural agency which brought it about. So, for instance, early man said that thunder was caused by a god shaking his spear. Now we explain it in terms of charged particles under the influence of air currents, etc. This satisfies us until we put the search further and further back, and ask what caused the charged particles to behave as they do and so on. One of the arguments of the present enquiry is to suggest that we are now at a position of this kind with regard to our desire to explain the origins of the universe and of our existence. We have arrived satisfactorily at the Big Bang, so many billions of years ago, and we have a relatively reasonable system of explanations as to how things developed from then on. However, we have, at present, no satisfactory explanation of what happened before and what caused the Big Bang to happen. We may hope to push our enquires further back and get nearer to some explanations in response to these questions, but meanwhile we seem to need a myth to satisfy our wish to know how they happen. It would, of course, be possible just to say that we do not know the answers to these questions, or even that it is impossible to know the answers to the questions because our minds, like the rest of us, were created at the Big Bang and they are formed in such a way that they can only operate on the categories of space and time which also have their origins at that moment.

But there may be many people who are reluctant to accept this limitation to enquiry, and would prefer to have a non-rational explanation rather than no explanation at all. We could, in any case, perhaps agree amongst these two schools of thought that the limitation of our powers of scientific exploration is temporary, and that on the extension of them beyond their present limits, we can do away with some – or indeed all – of the myths.

Another cause for myth-making in our earlier history was the perceived need to explain what happens within ourselves, as well as externally. Here again there seemed to be elements that were not susceptible to rational explanations, when powerful, and at first sight, inexplicable influences took command of the human emotions, as in the case, for example, of drunkenness, love and insanity. So people felt they had to invent myths to account for these happenings and, in classical mythology, they invented gods of wine and love, Bacchus and Venus, and thought of the insane as possessed by devils. The need for the myth has subsequently declined as in the case of the physical world, with the analysis of human psychology and physiology. Venus and the Devil have to some extent given way to Freud and Jung. Bacchus has given way to the drink-driving laws.

This mythological superstructure has gradually been peeled away as the natural causes of events are discovered one after another. It is the purpose of scientific enquiry to push this frontier back further and further to increase the area covered by reason, and to reduce the area which is not yet amenable to it. We cannot yet tell whether it will be possible to push this process forwards eventually covering everything of which we are aware in the world, and to bring all phenomena into a scientific framework.

At present we are short of achieving this goal in several respects. One of the most important is that we are, at present, unable to say on a scientific basis what happened before the Big Bang, and what will happen after the end of the material universe. We have the choice of either saying that such questions are unanswerable, and will always remain so, or of thinking of a temporary myth which we can imagine in order to provide an explanation, albeit a non-rational one for these aspects of the world around us which are not yet amenable to scientific rules. But there are several important differences between modern myth-making, if we accept that such is necessary, and the myths of old. Firstly, we do not have to believe that our myths are permanent. On the contrary, we will hope that, as science progresses, the area to be left to myth becomes smaller and smaller. Secondly, we can limit our myths to the minimum necessary to provide for the, at present inexplicable, elements in our system, rather than provide, as in many of the world's religions, that the supernatural elements which we are forced to imagine are all-powerful and have influence over all aspects of our life. Thirdly, there is no need to attribute to whatever beings or entities we feel bound to imagine, the desire or power to impose moral or ethical standards on our behaviour. This also has been a characteristic of the myths previously invented by most of the world's religions. We are therefore in search of a minimalist myth, concordant with some styles of modern architecture.

We are attempting here to indicate some of the points at which scientific exploration has so far failed to provide the answers, and for which we may therefore, if we wish, try to devise some mythic explanation and to suggest kinds of myth which might be appropriate, but we are suggesting that the mythic element in our appreciation of the world should be of the smallest possible character, unlike previous myth-makers who delighted in the proliferation of gods and goddesses and devils to whom they seemed often to devote a poetic imagination, rather than the rigours of scientific doctrine. Of course if others prefer a more poetic or artistic elaboration of the myths, which may be still necessary today, they are at liberty to create them.

One of the beauties of the mythic explanation of the remaining unsolved conundrums of the universe is that there is no means of judging whether they are true or false. Speculation can take its own way. The artistic and literary treasures, which have derived from earlier myths, show that there can be spin-offs in other spheres of human activity. There is no need to despise the myth-making capability of human beings, just because the myth is basically the result of a failure of reason in reaching its goals. We are free to indulge our myth-making, provided always that we do not insist that our myths are fundamentally true, and that anyone who does not believe them has to be treated as an unbeliever or heretic.

Why do we wish to insist upon the mythical element in the universe being restricted in scope in the way suggested above? There are several reasons. Firstly, it is difficult to conceive that the universe – as we know it – should have been constructed by an all-powerful and all-wise entity. It has so many inefficiencies, so much waste. Secondly, it is even more difficult on this basis than on others to account for the contrast between the apparent timelessness of what happened before, and what will happen after, and of what entity started the whole thing off, with the time-bound condition of our universe and our life – of this more below. Thirdly, the attempt to create myths on this basis of all-powerfulness, and especially when accompanied with the belief in the same entity being all-wise and benevolent, have led to the most terrible results as witnessed by the history of at least the three most prominent monotheistic religions of our time: Judaism, Christianity and Islam. It is highly undesirable that, if we are creating a new myth, we should fall into the same delusions of grandeur which accompanied most of the previous ones and which lead – almost invariably – to exclusivity and wars between rival religions or sects.

On the first point, the current descriptions of our universe include the picture of innumerable galaxies rushing away from each other in headlong flight at almost unimaginable speeds and distances. We are endowed with a feeling of purpose, and it is therefore difficult, if not impossible, for us to conceive of any enterprise being carried out without a purpose. The creation of a universe with rules which cause this dispersal of galaxies to happen must seem excessively purposeless. Similarly, at the other end of the scale of size we are confronted with a more or less unintelligible theory of the smallest elements of matter. The Greeks thought of matter as composed of indissoluble atoms, which is more or less intelligible by common sense and can be more or less visualised. But since this was found to be inadequate as a means of predicting how matter would behave, and the present menagerie of sub-atomic particles was invented, some of which have a life of only a few nano-seconds, and all of which are quite invisible to the naked eye, and since their behaviour is decided by quantum mechanics, which again has many elements which are repugnant to common sense, it is difficult to believe that this degree of complexity was really necessary or contributes to any purposeful structure.

The only purposeful element which we know of in the universe, is ourselves. So do we have to accept the anthropic principle that the whole thing was designed in order to produce us? Or, to put it another way, that since we are the only things that we know, we cannot fully explain or see the purpose of other parts of the system which appear to have nothing to do with our existence? In this category seem to fall the dispersing galaxies and the intricacies of sub-atomic matter. If, as seems likely, given our inherent belief in purpose, that we are the only things which it was worthwhile to create because we are the only things having purpose, then surely it would have been possible to produce this result without all the amazingly extravagant superstructure and infrastructure of the galaxies and quantum mechanics. Presumably we had to have the

Big Bang in order to produce the elements, out of which we – and the world surrounding us – are composed, but the other galaxies and the manner in which they are rushing away from each other, were accidental concomitants of the main line of development which led to ourselves. While the Big Bang on this line of thought may have been conditioned, or given rules likely to have the effect of producing something like ourselves, it may have been a necessary consequence of the way this was done that the other galaxies were created and behave as they do, and that matter had to be of the kind that modern physical theory would have us believe it is. In this case, we have to say that these accompaniments of the main purpose of the Big Bang and the rules which the universe subsequently followed were necessary for creating the system in which we now find ourselves.

It may well be, of course, that we are not the only experiments which exist. It may be that, in some or all of the other galaxies, or in other places in this one, other experiments are being conducted with slightly different rules. In that case it may have been part of the original plan that the other galaxies should be produced, in order to provide the locale in which these experiments can take place. It may also be that the theories of the sub-atomic particles and quantum mechanics are necessary in order to provide the framework for the concept of other universes, which we shall see is one way of providing for a solution to the difficulty between timelessness and our time-bound existence. But apart from this possibility, it is difficult to see why the extraordinary complexity of sub-atomic matter should be necessary in order to produce conditions in which it is possible for a race of intelligent and purposeful beings to prosper. If these components of our system are accidental or capricious, this must throw light on the nature of whoever or whatever pressed the button to bring about the Big Bang and laid down the rules, which would be followed by all subsequent developments.

We have already touched on the problem of reconciling timelessness and time, and we will develop thoughts on this further in a later chapter. The remaining difficulty is that the myths which assume the existence of all-powerful gods, as represented in today's world largely by Judaism, Christianity and Islam, have resulted in a lethal division between those who believe in one sort of god of this kind, and those who believe in other sorts – and these quarrels are not only between the religions, but also largely, and with equally disastrous consequences, within each religion in which adherents to particular interpretations of the myth consider that they alone are right, and have the duty to convert or exterminate those who do not accept their interpretations.

The Old Testament is full of stories of the Jews attacking those other inhabitants of Palestine who were not Jews, until finally they were carried off in captivity to Babylon, just because they were Jews. Christianity produced the heretic very early in its history, and continued to persecute those who were not of the same sect as themselves until very late in history, and indeed the results of the sectarian divide are still visible in Ireland. Islam was spoilt from near its beginning by the division into Sunni and Shia. It went though a period of tolerance in the middle ages and the early modern periods, but has since, in many cases, relapsed into fundamentalism and intolerance of those who criticise it, or fail to adopt the same religious and social rules which, for example, the Taliban propound. All this sad history suggests that faith in an all powerful being leads to exclusivity and to conflict between those who believe in a particular doctrine, and those who do not. This is a good reason for us to avoid dogma in our myth, and to ascribe the very minimum powers to any entities which we have to invent, either in our search for protection from some higher level of being, or as an explanation of those things in our experience for which we cannot yet find a rational explanation. The upshot is that in the present state of our knowledge, we seem to be forced to make a hypothesis about an external entity as the agency through which the whole process of the Big Ban began, leading to the existence of the universe as we know it and, since our minds are conditioned to require that an action must be carried out with a purpose, it is tempting to conclude that the purpose of beginning this process was to produce purposeful beings, namely ourselves. But there is no need to assume a purpose in all the rest of the universe, much of which seems to us to be pointless, and we may therefore regard it as the accidental concomitant of the process which led to the creation of purposeful beings. If this is so, it would be natural to think that the process may be regarded as an experiment, and the entity which brought it about as the experimenter. The bits left over, like the receding galaxies, could then be regarded as the accidental consequences of the process, or as a whimsical addition to it. It seems to be mainly a matter for personal choice whether we should regard the experimenter as not having complete control of the consequences of his experiment or as having a whimsical point of view which led to the extravagances which are found at the top and bottom ends of the scale of the universe as we perceive it. The possibility of doing without moral imperatives in this process, and therefore of avoiding the penalties of exclusivity and conflict which have resulted from them throughout the history of religion, is developed further in a later chapter which suggests that moral behaviour can be derived simply from prudential rules about behaviour between members of the human race designed to make life easier and more pleasurable, as described in the history of humanism.

In other words, science gives us only a very imperfect picture of the world and, when we ask some of these big questions about it, we are left with a choice between four alternatives: one is to say that science will find the answers to these questions one day, meanwhile because there is no answer it is not worth asking the questions. Secondly, we could say that it all happened by chance anyway, and that there is therefore no point in looking for a rational answer. Thirdly, we may be told that science will never disclose the ultimate mysteries of life, and that we must leave a place for these to be dependent on the creation of the universe by some supernatural being. Finally, we can say that, since we are imbued by nature with an overwhelming spirit of scientific enquiry, we have to go on looking for scientific explanations, but meanwhile it may be found convenient and respond to another aspect of our make-up that we should invent a myth to explain what science cannot explain.

There used to be an argument for the existence of God based on the analogy of the watchmaker. If you look at a watch with all its complex and usually successful mechanism, you are bound to conclude that this was made by an intelligent and creative being. Similarly, when you look at the world, you see a larger-scale mechanism, which works more or less, and which is of such complexity that it demands the assumption of an all-powerful entity which put it together. One of the purposes of this enquiry is to suggest what might be the nature of a myth, if one is required in our present state of ignorance of many of the basic questions about the universe and, if so, what kind of myth it should be? It will be suggested that the alleged necessity for myth is unfortunate, and may be of limited duration, and that any enquiry into it should be guided by the principle already suggested in the 14th century as the rule of 'ontological economy', to the effect that 'entities are not to be multiplied beyond necessity'. Following this rule, it may well be that it would be wrong for us to try to explain everything. The extravagances of modern cosmological theory and of quantum mechanics do not necessarily have to be viewed as apart of the scheme of things. They could be regarded as accidental accretions to what may have been the main purpose of what has happened, or they may be the result of whim.

It is part of our make-up to believe that things are done for a purpose. The only purposeful thing of which we are aware in the universe which we see around us is ourselves. There is a large element of accident in the stages that led to the production of the world as we now see it, with all its apparent wastefulness and absurdity. It was suggested long ago that the only satisfactory description of God was as an unsuccessful artist. It now looks as if it might be more appropriate to describe whoever was responsible for this state of affairs as a whimsical mathematician.

Chapter 2

Time and the Timeless

We have to consider what sort of subjects should be covered by our myth (because they are inexplicable by present scientific knowledge) and what kind of myth it has to be to cover these subjects. One of the more difficult subjects is this one relating to time. We exist in a system that has a beginning and will have an end, so far as we can at present foresee. It began with the Big Bang and will end, either with the Big Crunch, or with a cold death with the exhaustion of energy supplies in the universe. But if we try to think what happened before and what will happen after, we are led to believe that both these conditions will be timeless and, presumably, of infinite duration. On the traditional religious theories, the maker of the universe was a timeless being outside the confines of time (and presumably space as we know it). On our minimalist hypothesis the experimenter, who pressed the button for the whole thing to begin, must be thought to have a similar situation of being outside the time of the finite system of which we are aware. It is often said, for example, that not only the material world, but also time and space, began at the Big Bang. They would presumably end at the Big Crunch. Whether they would also, at some period, end in the event of the cold death of an ever-expanding or static universe is a matter that has not received similar attention. The problem lies in considering the relationship of the originator of the present system as a being in a timeless condition, and the time-bound system of the universe. It is perhaps not so difficult to think of the position in terms of our 'Experimenter'. He could decide to try the experiment which produced our system, and when it comes to an end he could equally decide to try another one. If the universe is thought of on lines more consistent with conventional religion as being a single unique creation, it is more difficult to see the point of an eternal god creating something which is going to come to an end.

In other words, we have to try to reconcile the apparent timelessness of 'the before and after' and therefore presumably of whatever actually caused the universe to begin, with the time-bound system in which we exist. On a somewhat more personalised theory of origin, we may ask why a timeless being or entity should have decided to create an existence which was going to come to an end in this way. It would be argued that perhaps the experimenter himself need not be absolutely timeless, but this is merely putting the puzzle further back and involves thinking what happened before and after him.

We have noted above some of the examples of gods who came to an end, sometimes followed by resurrection. In the Christian myth, the life of Christ on earth had a beginning and an end, but after resurrection he entered or re-entered a timeless sphere, expected to be of infinite duration. So the differentiation remains between the timeless god and the time-bound human allegedly created by the timeless god.

We have two possibilities to consider as ways of escaping from this contradiction. One is to see how far we can put off, or escape from, the ending of the material circumstances, which are necessary for the continuation of our material life. The other is to ask whether there is some part of us that partakes of a non-material existence and which might therefore continue after the end of the material world.

To look first at our situation in the material world, there is a series of possible events which could bring life to an end, listed here in ascending order of danger. We could destroy our world in the comparatively near future, either by nuclear war or by pollution. The avoidance of these dangers is clearly within our grasp if we devote sufficient priority to achieving it. The next danger, on which no date can be set but could be quite early or much later, is the collision of the earth with a comet or asteroid which could cause such damage to the earth that it might make life temporarily or even terminally impossible. This would be a repetition of the disaster that overtook the earth some tens of millions of years ago, and was sufficiently serious to destroy the dinosaurs. There is no reason why it should not be possible to find means of avoiding this particular class of danger. We could perfect, by methods already available, the listing of other objects within or approaching the solar system and plot their probable courses in relation to the earth. Having done so, we could surely devise means of sending missiles to intercept these bodies in such a way as to divert their course if they threatened to hit the earth. This might require the devotion of greater resources than would at present be available to achieve these ends, also a higher degree of international cooperation than is usually experienced. But the extension of ideas like 'Star Wars' from systems to defeat missiles coming from other countries to those coming from space is not beyond the bounds of present or foreseeable science, provided that enough resources are devoted to it.

The next categories of disaster are of a different character, in that it seems at present that it is most unlikely that we could find means of preventing their happening. The first in time would be changes in our sun that would make life no longer possible on the earth. The present forecast is that in something like six billion years, the sun becomes a red giant which would first fry us and then relapses into a dead star with no energy left to keep us alive, even if we had survived the first stage, which is highly improbable.

We can, theoretically, avoid this disaster by moving ourselves, or some of us, to the planet of another sun. Statistically, it is probable – with the vast number of stars in our galaxy – that some would have planets on which the conditions might be somewhat similar to our own. In fact, it seems that astronomers have detected planets in orbit round other stars, but so far without determining accurately what the conditions might be like. A great deal more research would be needed before we could find a suitable new home of this kind. Bearing in mind the very long period which will elapse before we have to make a move, it could well be that we could, by that time, have techniques available which would help us to modify the environment of another planet to make it more suitable for our descendants to live there. But even if we can find a suitable new home and do the necessary work on making it habitable, we are left with the question of how we could get there in a reasonable length of time. The reasons why such a journey is so difficult are first, the vast distances of interstellar space and, secondly, the limitation of movement in the universe to the speed of light. This latter principle was laid down by Einstein and appears at the present to be impregnable, at least so far as the movement of significant amounts of matter is concerned. There are rumours of tachyons, particles that can move faster than the speed of light, and there is the apparent possibility of photons (the basic units of light) behaving in a non-local way so that one can influence another at any distance without any apparent interval of time. These two apparent exceptions to Einstein's rule may be of the utmost importance with regard to the possibility of signalling between ourselves and other regions of the universe (if we find anyone to receive the signals), but that is a very different matter to the transport by material means of human beings. It looks at present, therefore, as though one would have to think in terms of space stations in which people could live for more than one generation in order to accomplish the journey to another possible planetary home. Here we are delving deep into the realms of space fiction, but so much of what was previously regarded as falling within this category has subsequently come true, that it should not necessarily be excluded for that reason. An attempt was described in the film *2001* to get round this problem by deep-freezing people on board a space ship with the idea that they would be 'defrosted' at the appropriate moment as they were approaching another planet on which they could live. In the film, the robot that was controlling the spacecraft on its journey, unfortunately decided to take it over, with catastrophic results. Depending on the time which one might think these processes will take to perfect, there would have to be a concerted use of resources in a way that is at present difficult to imagine, lasting over very long periods of time in order to bring such events about. With 6 billion years to go, there is probably enough time and there are likely to be scientific and mechanical developments during that time of kinds which we can hardly yet begin to imagine. Nevertheless, it seems that it may well be desirable to put down a marker to the effect that some efforts of this kind will be necessary if the human race is to overcome the demise of the sun, in a way that will prolong its existence by finding another sun with a longer life, not excluding the possibility that the process could be repeated a large number of times. The question of moving outside our own galaxy would multiply the problem by an enormous factor, owing to the increased distances and speeds with which the galaxies are moving away from each other. However, provided the techniques are developed, the scenario need not be excluded.

The final threat to the continued existence of the human race is the ending of the universe as a whole. Opinions among physicists and astronomers differ as to how this will come about. If the inertia of the galaxies continues to overcome the force of gravity, then they will continue to move away from each other into ever more distant areas of space-time. But they will at the same time be using up all the energy that they now contain by the normal processes of the evolution of stars which, so far as we can judge, do not contain infinitely renewable resources of energy. On the other main theory, the force of gravity eventually overcomes the centrifugal motions of the galaxies, and they will all start moving towards each other, finally ending in the Big Crunch when they will merge once again into unimaginably small concentrations of matter, similar to what preceded the Big Bang. This would, of course, be equally inimical to the continuation of life as we know it. Another view is occasionally heard that the final outcome will be neither of these two scenarios, but a steady state in which the forces of movement and of gravity will reach an equilibrium, and the galaxies will continue to remain in the positions which they have attained at the point when this happens. But there is nothing to suggest that the steady state will be any better than the dispersing galaxies at maintaining or renewing its energy sources, and there would be nothing to look forward to but a gradual cooling, ending in a cold death of all matter in the universe.

It is, of course, possible to think that after the Big Crunch, everything could start all over again. The resulting concentration of matter in an incredibly small space would be similar to what is supposed to have taken place immediately prior to the Big Bang. So one could, theoretically, expect a succession of expanding universes followed by crunches followed by Big Bangs. Such a picture would go quite well with the analogy of the Experimenter, which we have put forward as one of the hypotheses for what takes place before and after the material universe. An experiment such as we are now undergoing could well be succeeded by another experiment in which the rules might be slightly different, so that a different evolution might result. It could even be that the series of experiments would be designed to produce a system which would have longer and possibly infinite duration, and so match the conditions of the experimenter. We could thus imagine having a succession of universes, some of which might produce conditions similar to the one we know, and others which might be conducive to the creation of life forms different from ours but having a similar kind of discrete existence. It will be difficult to prove or disprove a hypothesis of this kind. What we can know is that *we*, the present inhabitants of this universe, are faced with the problem of our own survival.

To recapitulate the problem: why should something timeless bring about a system like our universe that has a beginning and an end? Most answers are unsatisfactory .The timeless element which we are assuming may not, in fact, be timeless; we have seen some mythical examples in which the end of the god or gods is foreseen, sometimes followed by resurrection. This is not very different from saying that we are an experiment, to be followed, after our ending, by another experiment – and so on *ad infinitum* if you wish. One of the troubles with this line of thought is that if we insist that actions must be purposeful, then we need to speculate about the purpose of this series of experiments, and the criteria by which to judge whether they are successful. An experiment, after all, is designed either to prove or to discover a truth. What is our timeless entity looking for? Escape from boredom? Renewal of itself or its species? Company? Find something else purposeful? Or a new range of timeless beings?

It is alleged that time itself, like all material things, originated at the Big Bang, and that it is therefore impossible to ask, far less answer, the question of what happened before the Big Bang. In a state without time the word before has no meaning. This is exceptionally hard for us to take in, but the alternative, being able to write a history of what went before, is equally difficult. Constituted as we are, it is equally impossible for us not to say that an event happened, apparently requiring an initiative to bring it about. Even if we try to escape this idea of motivation by saying it was just chance, we still need some way in which the rules of probability originated. It is hard enough to think of nothing, but worse still to think how we came out of it, by chance, inventing purpose on the way.

Leaving these weighty questions for the moment, the question could well be asked: 'Why should we make such enormous efforts to provide for the survival of the human race or, at best, probably a small part of it, in the face of the cosmological catastrophes which we anticipate, particularly if, in the end, such efforts are going to be useless because the whole of the material universe, including ourselves will inevitably come to an end?' There are two main reasons why we should do this. One is a kind of ethical consideration; the other a response to an instinctive urge. On the ethical side, we are the only beings which we know of which have a purpose, and we claim to be superior to other kinds of life. We have managed to survive disasters successfully in the past, like the ice age and various diseases. We should consider it a duty, consonant with our claims to superiority, that we should continue to seek to exist and improve the quality of our lives. *Noblesse oblige*, in other words. Whether or not it is related to any such sense of duty we also clearly have a very strong instinctive urge to survive. There have no doubt been occasions in the distant past when our openness to accept one course or one possibility or opportunity has contributed to the prolongation and development of the human race. The acceptance of the Neolithic farming revolution, leading ultimately to civilisation as we know it, may be one of these of which we can have some archaeological awareness. Resistance to totalitarianism, as demonstrated in the Second World War, might be considered another such moment of decision. The decision whether or not to devote enormous resources to the effort to move to another planet in order to avoid the death of the sun will be another such decisive moment in which our urge to provide for survival, even of a small part of the human race, is likely to be predominant.

Chapter 3

Non-material survival: The Intelligent Machine

With the prospects for material survival as bleak as they appear to be, given the ultimate ending of the universe as a whole, it is natural that we should look at other possibilities of survival, which do not depend on the persistence of the material world. One of the these is the familiar picture of the survival of spirits emanating from material people, but endowed with a continuing – and often assumed to be eternal – life in a spirit world separate from the material world. The other possible method, much less familiar, is the idea of the creation of intelligent machines that could continue to exist after their creators no longer existed. To deal with this latter possibility – the argument whether or not it is possible to create an artificial intelligence – has been active for many years. It depends partly, of course, on what you mean by 'intelligence'. Can the programme escape from the programmer?

This possibility was aired in a television programme in December 1999, which described how SETI (Search for Extra Terrestrial Intelligence) finally received a signal which denoted that it had been transmitted by an intelligent being elsewhere in the universe. After complicated mathematical calculations, it emerged that this being was transmitting a picture of itself. After arousing world-wide alarm, and then intense world-wide interest, it turned out that the picture, when eventually de-coded, was that of a very complicated intelligent machine, without any clue as to who had created it. The suggestion was made that this could be the ultimate result of the search which is already going on for intelligent computers, one of the first tasks to be given to such a machine being to produce a still more intelligent version of itself, and with the final idea that once a certain stage in this process had been reached, there could be machines which had their own independent life. The importance of this kind of machine would be that it could travel about the universe independently, having no need for a space-suit or other means of survival in the unfriendly environment of space, but could exist simply by replenishing its energy store which it could do, no doubt, at various points in the universe, drawing on supplies of energy readily available in dust or planets. This would not provide for survival beyond the time when the universe itself came to an end, either in the crunch or by using up all its energy supplies and relapsing in to a cold and infinite series of masses. A further stage in the idea might be to examine whether the necessary comparatively small amounts of energy required to keep such a machine going could be obtained from the generalised radiation which is present throughout the universe, derived from the radiation left over from the Big Bang. This radiation is uniform throughout the universe, but is of exceedingly low power. Nevertheless, it is capable of producing a hum in electrical equipment, which means that it can operate on electrical receiving apparatus and produce work by causing an audible signal. It might not be beyond the powers of future scientists to channel this energy somehow, and use it to provide for the survival of intelligent machines, and there would be a question as to whether this generalised radiation would continue to exist after the death of the universe, with whose creation it had been associated.

To push this speculation even further beyond the realms of fact, there could be the fascinating idea that such intelligences exist already, having been created by more advanced civilisations in other parts of the universe, and perhaps one of them was programmed to seek a suitable place to recreate an earlier civilisation such as had created it, and that this is the origin of our own world. This does not provide an answer to the question of origins, since it does not explain how the earlier civilisation originated. At least it would interpose an earlier civilization plus a creation of artificial intelligences between us and the beginning of the experiment. One could imagine that the intelligence which led to our beginning, was developed by an earlier civilisation in circumstances like those which we foresee for ourselves, namely the anticipated extinction of their sun or energy source.

It would be going even further, into what may only be described as the absurd, to suppose that an artificial intelligence could, if sufficiently developed, be a much more elemental root of our existence, namely as creating the Big Bang itself. This might, however, help to explain the extraordinary and apparently purposeless extensions of our world at both ends which we have already discussed, namely the proliferation and dispersal of apparently useless galaxies and the unwarranted complication at the other end of the scale in the subatomic world of quantum mechanics, etc. It is somewhat more acceptable to believe that an artificial intelligence could indulge in these vagaries than a timeless entity of a more personal kind.

The other possible means of non-material survival, which may well be more worthwhile investigating than the science fiction of the last few paragraphs, is that which supposes that there is an element in us which is of a non-material character. This is what is normally described as the spirit or soul and manifests itself in psychic experiences of various kinds, which, in so far as they may be genuine, take place outside the normal bounds of science and are therefore rejected by many orthodox scientists.

Chapter 4

Survival: The Spirit World

We have therefore to consider the whole question of the relationship between the material and non-material parts of the cosmos. When Descartes uttered his famous maxim: *Cogito ergo sum* – I think, therefore I am – he left it sadly incomplete. I am what? Is the part of me that thinks and says 'I am', independent of the material world? Is it tautologous: I think therefore there is an I that thinks? Does it mean that I, as a person having a material body, exist or simply that some disembodied mind exists? Do minds, spirits, or whatever you like to call them have to have bodies attached to them? We only know that the mind is there because people say so through material means, whether by writing or speaking. On the other hand, there are examples in which minds seem to be able to operate independently of body or material means of communication, as in telepathy. A great many people, perhaps the majority, accept that transference of thought can come about occasionally without any material means that can be observed, and we call this telepathy. It can happen between human beings and, as recently proved by Rupert Sheldrake, between human beings and animals, and probably between animals themselves. (Serious arguments have now been put forward against this view).

The acceptance of telepathy, even though it seems to many people almost commonplace, implies the existence of communicators and recipients operating in a non-material way, and not by any means of signalling which has, up to now, been detectable.

We might note here that those who do not accept personal survival usually say that the veridical communications of mediums are the result of telepathy with the sitter, as if this disposed of the existence of a non-material factor, whereas in fact telepathy is almost as mysterious as personal survival. It is no good objecting to this notion by saying that the non-material element cannot exist because it does not obey the rules of space-time. On the contrary, it is only of interest to us in this context *because* of this characteristic. If space and time originated at the Big Bang, they must presumably end at the crunch or the black hole. What we are at present seeking is to see whether there is an element in our make-up which can continue after normal space and time have come to an end, with the death of the universe. Only if it has this character can we overcome the difficulty of a timeless being creating or originating something bound by time. There is no evidence of a falling-off of the strength of a telepathic signal due to distance, and there appears to be no time interval in its transmission, any more than there is in our projecting our thought or visualising the sun and stars.

What we are investigating is whether there is, in our experience of consciousness, a feeling of something outside the normal bodily circumstances, looking in at them from some position outside or independent, and whether telepathy and other psychical manifestations prove that parts of ourselves can operate outside the normal rules pertaining to matter. If a spiritual element within us, attached to us in some way, operates outside the normal limits of space-time, then it is almost logical that it can continue after the ending of space-time, which is likely to occur with the ending of the material universe. This would, to some extent, resolve the paradox of the timeless entity, giving rise to a time-bound world, since it would appear that this world could, in its turn, give rise to something timeless.

To many people faced with the question whether there is a non-material element in the world which can survive the end of the material element, it would seem more natural to consider the question in relation to alleged manifestations of personal survival such as ghosts, or the communications allegedly made between living persons and the dead through mediums, etc. If ghosts exist, they should presumably be thought of as existing outside the ordinary rules of time and space as we know them, and therefore having potentially unlimited future existence. On the other hand, it could be asked whether ghosts could be there unless there had been a physical counterpart to them in the material world. We talk of disembodied spirits, but it would usually be thought that these occurred, if they do, as a consequence of having been at an earlier stage embodied. Another aspect of ghost lore is that such apparitions are normally thought to be associated with places or buildings. It is as if people or events in which they were involved were somehow able to stamp on pieces of material (stone walls etc) traces of some kind of memory, which can be tapped into by those with sufficient psychic powers, even at a much later date. If anything like this is the case then it would make it even more unlikely that ghosts could exist without some previous material association. So that, if matter comes to an end, there would be no more material objects for ghosts to attach themselves to. So would there be no more ghosts?

It is no good just saying that ghosts are the result of hallucination, as if this settled the matter. We need to know what triggers the hallucination, and why, for example in a ghost story about a haunted house, the trigger appears to operate in a particular locality. Here again we are faced with a phenomenon which is not amenable to physical measurement, except to the extent that there are fairly often reports of a lowering of the ambient temperature accompanying the sighting of ghosts. This is sometimes interpreted as the withdrawal of energy from the surroundings in order to power the manifestation of the apparition, but again by means which are not susceptible to measurement. If any of this is true, we are faced, as in telepathy, with occurrences having a decisive non-material input, and which manifest themselves through the senses or depend on material means of expression for their communication. It is the non-material element which prompts us to speculate that there may be something involved in such occurrences which is not contained within normal space-time.

Another curious speculation is available about the persistent autonomy of a non-material entity. In a particularly opaque but potentially fruitful passage of *Le Temps Retrouvé*, Proust suggests that a memory may fall into this category .The memory of a long past event, of a sight or sound, may introduce itself into present consciousness for no reason at all and with no apparent relation to what is occupying the consciousness at the later time. The particular memory which does this seems to repeat itself by chance, unless there is some deep unconscious motivation at work.

This train of thought could perhaps have some similarity to Jung's synchronicity by which meaningful coincidental events happen for no apparent reason, somehow attracted by similarity or identity of apparently unrelated objects or happenings. In other words there is some influence out there which can bring about events independently of the usual limitation of cause and effect.

These rather marginal and speculative considerations are mentioned here because they may somewhat blur the distinction we have suggested between the time-bound world of our normal surroundings, and the timeless state presumed to exist before and after the existence of our present world.

But to many people the more significant – and incidentally the most desirable – form of the survival of a non-material element of our world would be that of survival of the spirits or souls of dead persons. And a great deal of effort is put into the attempt to prove that this exists by means of communication through mediums.

The Society for Psychical Research was set up over 100 years ago with the main object of proving whether or not such personal survival takes place. Regrettably, in spite of heroic efforts, there has not been any evidence produced which unambiguously convinces the majority of people that this is the case. It is, for example, notoriously difficult to determine whether the utterances of mediums alleged to be coming from deceased persons have, in fact, been derived by the medium by telepathy from the sitter. In some cases, this hypothesis itself presents such great difficulties that recourse has to be had to the idea of generalised telepathy by which the medium can tap into the minds or memories of anyone else in the world. In such cases, it can almost be argued that to accept survival is a simpler hypothesis and should therefore be adopted.

What do we mean by survival? We have several models available: the Greeks in Homer's time envisaged the after-life in Hades as populated by shades of formerly living people, recognisable and able to communicate, at any rate with a privileged visitor like Odysseus, but not at all enjoying the after-life. Achilles said that he would rather live as a slave in somebody's household on earth than be ruler of the Shades. The early Arabs envisaged paradise as a garden inhabited by beautiful maidens, where the souls of those killed in fighting the infidels were translated. The assassins were fed with hashish ('assassin' is derived from '*hashishin*' = those under the influence of hashish) to give them a foretaste of what it would be like. Nordic mythology had a somewhat similar picture of dead heroes being transported to Valhalla by the beautiful female Valkyries. The Christians had the more jejune picture of the souls of the righteous sitting on clouds playing the harp, while the souls of the unrighteous suffered torments in hell. The Buddhists, on the contrary, saw the soul migrating from one person to another, ending up, if you were particularly good, in the state of nothingness known as Nirvana. The son of Oliver Lodge, who was killed in the First World War, told his father, through a medium, that in the afterlife where he was, cigars and whiskey and soda could be provided for those newly arrived spirits who asked for them, but they were not so good as the terrestrial varieties and people soon tired of them. (*Raymond Revisited* by Sir Oliver Lodge, Methuen, London, 1922.). So there is a wide choice of models.

If we wish to think of something emanating from us which can survive the end of the universe we must think of it as transcending matter, space and time, and therefore maybe not being energy, because $E = Mc^2$, that is to say energy must be expressible in terms of mass. Or do we have somehow to get behind that? Can we imagine a massless energy? If so, how does it express itself? In other words, what is the energy source for telepathy, and, even more, for poltergeist manifestations? Are we looking at another universe with different rules?

One of the problems is that we find it hard to imagine a timeless state, with no progression. What is the point of it? Does the soul learn, develop, grow? Is there a progression from one stage to another? Is there a hierarchy? This last point was put succinctly as early as the 17th century by Cudworth, a Cambridge Platonist, who wrote: 'If there be once any visible ghosts or spirits acknowledged as things permanent, it would not be easy for any to give a reason why there might not be one supreme ghost also presiding over them all and the whole world.' (I am indebted for this quotation to the book *Religion and the Decline of Magic* by Keith Thomas, Penguin London 1983).

We are examining these questions so as to see if we can think of an indefinitely prolonged life to match the alleged timelessness of the experimenter. But if timelessness necessarily implies being static, it is hardly a form of existence as we know it. So we may well have to leave the question open – being certain of only three things: firstly, that the universe will end; secondly, that until then we are here with an urge to continue our own life as long as possible, and thirdly, that there is a non-material part of us which we can at present not measure or explain, but which may have important consequences for our future existence in some form, but of such a nature as we cannot at present know.

We are pushed into agnosticism on this point by the very great difficulty which we have of imagining another kind of life which is not somehow in the image of the life that we know here. Sometimes it is imagined to be better, sometimes worse. But, to make sense to us as meaningful survival, it has at first sight to be in the form of the survival of discrete personalities, which we have to think of as pursuing a kind of existence similar in some ways at least to the existence of discrete personalities in this world. Particularly if, as suggested above, we have to think of the spiritual part of ourselves as existing, if at all, in a situation in which the categories of time and space as we know them do not apply, the kind of existence which we are trying to imagine must be so different, that it is hardly surprising that we have great difficulty in envisaging it.

Another consequence of this aspect of the nature of survival is that if we are right in thinking we have to imagine something taking place outside the categories of time and space as we know them, we are thinking of something which is at least in some ways in the same situation as the experimenter who, on the basis of the myth which we are attempting to define, also operates outside these categories. Can we deduce from this any idea that there might be communication between the spiritual parts of ourselves after bodily death and the experimenter, or any indications of what the nature of the experimenter may be? We have already insisted on one aspect of the definition, namely that the experimenter should be of a minimalist character. He is only required to press a button and transmit a set of rules about the development of the physical universe following on the Big Bang. Can we go beyond this minimalist definition and speculate about the nature of whatever it is that has to fulfil this role in our myth?

Even if we believe that survival takes place and that this can therefore offer us another avenue to escape the limits of material time and provide a means by which at least a non-material element related to us can last indefinitely, we run into the difficulty, with which we are already familiar: that the spirits – or whatever we like to call them – which survive are survivors from a person which we regard as being a material object, even though endowed with spiritual attributes. What happens when the supply of physical persons is exhausted? Does this mean the end of the production of new spirits since there will be no more material beings with which such spirits have normally been associated? This will impose a serious limitation on the content of the continued existence of the spirit world, since this will be filled with the spirits of those people who were in existence before the end of the material world without any renewal or supply of new spirits. So it would be impossible altogether to escape the idea of mortality even in a spirit world of this kind.

There is another curious anomaly in the concept of survival as commonly held. As stated above, there is good evidence to suggest that certain animals have a capability of telepathic communication with humans. Also, one has only watch a flock of starlings manoeuvring at dusk, or a school of fish avoiding pursuit in the ocean to believe that telepathic communication may also exist between animals in order to facilitate their uniform movements in these conditions. There are also plausible stories about animals having precognition of disasters. This would, in any case, be believed about some of the higher animals by those closely associated with them. Must we then assume that the non-material faculties which they possess could have a continuation of existence, even when the material parts of them cease to exist? But where do you draw the line? The only time I have consulted a medium, following on a bereavement, I was told that there was a dog accompanying the deceased person. If dogs, why not dinosaurs? Can we really envisage a heaven peopled by dinosaurs and microbes, and all the other creatures that have ever been in existence?

No less an authority than Martin Luther envisaged the survival of dogs when he said: 'Be comforted, little dog; thou too at the resurrection shall have a little golden tail.' It may also be recalled that in Greek mythology, passengers to the underworld – after the death of the body – were confronted by the dog Cerberus. However, he was a creature with three heads and therefore not a very close representation of the dog as household pet.

If we cannot accept the survival of animals, we are forced to the position of saying that man alone, through the possession of consciousness – whatever that may mean – has a spiritual element which can continue after bodily death. But when did this start? Was it possessed also by the Neanderthals, homo erectus and all the other forbears of homo sapiens?

We will consider later the question of other universes, and of living beings in other parts of this universe, but there is an interesting point about survival to which these possibilities give rise. There is no inherent reason why, if there are living and intelligent beings elsewhere than on this earth, they should not also have spiritual elements attached to them. If so, then they should also qualify for survival, and we have to envisage an afterlife, if any, filled with the spirits not only of human beings and animals but of 'little green men' as well. The religions would also get into a serious tangle if they thought seriously about this possibility. They claim that their revelations are universal, even though not everyone believes in them, but does this go for intelligent beings in other parts of the universe as well? Or are they expected to have their own revelation or myths? Christians believe that Christ came to earth to redeem the sins of human beings and promise them resurrection. Did he also visit other places where intelligent life exists? Or was there some other manifestation of the divine? It is easier for humanists (except that the name might have to be changed!). All they have to do is to apply the same principles of behaviour with aliens as they do with fellow human beings. Since they have no habit of exclusivity, it is no more difficult for them to enter into friendly and rational relations with aliens than with people of another race on earth.

It would, of course, be possible to believe that the spirits existed before the origination of the material world. Wordsworth possibly had something like this in mind when he wrote of us coming into the world 'trailing clouds of glory'. If something like this were the case, it would be possible to believe that the spirits had a timeless origin and were only tied to time and space in so far as they manifest themselves to us through material means, as a temporary interval in their otherwise timeless existence. This might then pose the question why they were to be subjected to this material phase unless that was thought to allow them to participate in a more meaningful society than they otherwise enjoy, and to go through processes of experience and growth which were not available to them in their non-material form. One would have the difficult task of imagining a 'free spirit' or a group of such spirits feeling dissatisfied or bored with their non-material existence and deciding to subject themselves as an experiment to the task of inspiring, or in some way adding themselves to a race of material beings whose experiences could in some form be more dramatic, testing, or poignant than those which they enjoyed in a non-material form. This may be regarded as a particularly far-out concept, but just remember that the question of origins is, in any case, so difficult that it should not necessarily be excluded on these grounds alone.

None of this speculation is particularly helpful to the ordinary person's search for evidence of the personal survival of a loved one. But it is this yearning itself – and the difficulty of satisfying it – that may drive us to other concepts. When one of a couple of people who have had a strong or overriding personal relationship dies, it is very hard to believe that, if there is any survival at all, this relationship must come to an end. The feelings for the other must continue after death. But the evidence for their doing so is so unsatisfactory that the idea of personal survival almost has to be abandoned.

To repeat, if there is personal survival, it is to a large extent unacceptable that the only communications between those who have had this kind of relationship are either the expression of feelings by the living, deriving from wish fulfilment, or the usually inane or suspect imaginings of mediums.

The difficulties about the idea of personal survival are so great that some people are led into thinking about a different scenario, namely that the spirit element of our existence merges after material death in a union of some kind. One version of the theories of this kind would be the collective unconscious of Jung. This seems to be a temporary repository of spirits or souls, which each individually contribute to the formation of the collectivity, and from which suitable parts are taken to provide the spirit for a new individual.

Metempsychosis, or the transfer of one soul to a person in a later generation – otherwise known as reincarnation – could be regarded as a sub-species of the general concept of a collective unconscious. The soul of a deceased person would not merge, or not merge immediately, into a collectivity in which its individuality would be lost, but could either occasionally – or often, or always – be transferred to a newly formed person, presumably of a later generation. Some people believe firmly that this happens, particularly in the Indian sub-continent, but there is by no means universal acceptance of this theory .Others who think it unsatisfactory to imagine that souls are put in a kind of filing cabinet to be taken out by chance or whim and re-used later, think instead that when the spirit departs from a living person it is merged in the whole, a union of all spiritual existence, and that this provides the only satisfactory goal for the future life of the spirit. Individuality is presumably lost, and this would provide the reason for which it is so difficult to obtain genuine communication between the living and the dead. But the tie of union with the whole is to be regarded as a greater goal even than the continuing existence of the individual.

It is naturally impossible to imagine how a theory of this kind could be verified. Therefore many people would find it as difficult to believe as the theory of personal survival. Moreover, this point of view does not seem to provide any answers to the question that, if this wholeness exists and has perhaps always existed and will continue in existence after the end of the material universe, why should our time-bound system have been created, being of such a very different nature from the idea of wholeness and union and having, on the contrary, so much indeed a predominant interest in the existence of the individual personality and its development? The attempt to answer this sort of question generally leads to ideas of the necessity of a progression through various stages in order to end up as partaking in the union, much on the lines of the Buddhist progression to Nirvana. And it is difficult to make an acceptable picture of this progression without introducing into it moral questions, or at least a system of values that gives greater reward to certain kinds of behaviour than to others, and so speeds the process from the individual personality to participation in the whole.

This seems to be straying a long way from the minimalist hypothesis with which we started the enquiry. It implies a greater degree of decision-making on the part of whoever created the whole set-up and is therefore undesirable from the point of view of our kind of myth-making. It seems also to give excessive power to those who set themselves up to interpret the theory by laying down codes of conduct which will lead, they say, to the desired results. We cannot say that this sort of idea is wrong, any more than the proponents of it can prove that it is right. It has to be left in the intellectually unsatisfying position of something, which can be believed either because somebody claims to have a mystical revelation to the effect that this is what happens or because we have run out of rational and intellectually acceptable alternatives.

It is strange that we exist in this world with a very strong sense of past, present and future, and a desire not only to know what the future holds, but also to continue to take part in it in some way, even when the material prospects of our continuing to exist indefinitely seem to be reduced to zero. It is strange, that is to say, that the various hypotheses which have been put forward to provide for some kind of non-material future all seem to be fraught with such difficulties and to be so lacking in evidence as to their truth or falsity .It is perhaps a complicated stratagem that has been played on us by our genes, because if we believed there was no future, it might be less worthwhile trying to continue to exist through all the difficulties that the human race has met, and that might bring about the ending of the race long before it is, in any case, going to cease in so many billion years. Therefore, we have to make the effort to survive – and, after all, if we survive long enough, there is always the chance that something may turn up. We must have the sense of a future extending in front of us and we must seek other means by which some part of us – perhaps the spiritual part – can continue to survive even when the material part of us will have ceased to do so. There could also be a question raised whether the genes, which have pushed us into imagining various kinds of future spiritual existence, would themselves take part in it. Whatever their wondrous capabilities, genes are presumably part of the material universe and it would seem difficult to imagine their continuing to exist after the end of that universe. Or do we have to believe that there could be a spiritual gene? But this would itself be illogical since we would be importing a system promoting change and progress or decline into an area which in other respects should be regarded as timeless.

Chapter 5

Aesthetics

There is another aspect of human personality which we have left out as falling perhaps halfway between material and immaterial or spiritual, namely the faculty of aesthetics. What help is it to our survival that we are powerfully influenced in our feelings by the beauty of a sunset or a picture or a person? And secondly, do the claims of artists that beauty or their expression of it is timeless or permanent relate to the existence in the natural world, or in the works of Man, of something that amounts to the existence of an entity that transcends time and space?

On the first question – does aesthetics promote survival? – there could be two contradictory answers. An appreciation of the beauty of a partner promotes the sexual act, which leads to procreation – at least in the higher animals – as demonstrated not only in human relations but in the courtship of peacocks, etc. This may be a necessary condition of the evolution of procreation from division, as in single-celled animals, to union between two elements, the egg and the sperm, carrying different gene counts, thus promoting variety and evolution.

On the other hand, if primitive men had stopped in the course of their mammoth hunt to admire the sunset, this would have been counterproductive to survival, as it would have given the mammoth a better chance to escape. But these same men, returning from their hunt, went back to their caves and decorated them with exquisite representations of their quarry. This is sometimes held to be magic, intended to make the hunt more successful or to propitiate the creatures whose lives were taken. Could the same be said about the origins of later art? Was the proliferation of images of the Mother Goddess designed to secure the continuation of the family or race? Was the painting of a pretty girl designed to increase the painter's chances in the same direction? The naughty rhyme about Titian suggests that it may sometimes have had this result, even though accidentally.

Later, was art intended to extract from the evidence of the senses some essence of form which could have a more enduring existence than the transient natural scene?

Since the beginning of writing there has been the same preoccupation to create something longer lasting than the author and the object of his writing, as various examples demonstrate. Horace wrote: *exegi monumentum aere perennius*, I have made a monument more lasting than bronze. Milton wrote of 'immortal verse'; Marlowe wrote of 'immortal flowers of poesy; Michael Drayton wrote 'I to thee eternity shall give.' And we should not forget that the members of the French Academy called themselves 'les immortels'. Robert Burns seems to have glimpsed the idea of post-universe immortality when he wrote:

Till a'the seas gang dry, my dear,
And the rocks melt wi' the sun,

quite an elegant description of the likely symptoms of the death of the sun, but rather spoiled the effect by adding, 'I will luve thee still, my dear,/While the sands of life shall run'. What we are talking about here is something that goes on after the sands of life (as we know it) have ceased to run.

So we are not short of claims that art can be immortal. The trouble is that the only means of expression so far as we know at present, depend on external, material means, which are not immortal. Therefore, if we are to achieve real immortality within the scheme of things which we are considering, we would be forced to say that the aesthetic sense is, or can be, or must be, part of the non-material or spiritual part of human beings, which we have sought to identify – or that all manifestations of beauty can be stored in intelligent machines, whose artificial memories may be able to survive the passing of the material universe.

Or perhaps there is another way of looking at this. Perhaps we should recognise that aesthetics are not given to us because it helps our survival, but on the contrary, that aesthetics – the power to create and appreciate beauty – are there for exactly the opposite reason, namely that they have nothing to do with survival. Wherever this faculty may come from it should on this view be regarded as something inherent in us in the same way that we have suggested there is a non-material or spiritual element in ourselves, and that this faculty is something that distinguishes us from other parts of creation and must be accounted for as a part of our overall make-up, which is not necessary for our survival, but is an accidental addition to the human condition. It is no doubt politically incorrect to say so, but the aesthetic sense seems to be something that distinguishes men from other living creatures. The only beauty inherent in other parts of the system is the appearance of some animals and plants, which, so far as we are at present able to judge, means that their beauty is appreciated by us. We have no means of knowing to what extent it is appreciated by them, except for the effect exercised by certain male animals on the females of the species which leads them to be chosen as mates, rather than those with an inferior display. The only artistic creation of which they are apparently capable is the intricate nests of certain birds, but these, perhaps partake more of the heading of craftsmanship rather than art for art's sake. Man, as so frequently expressed by poets and artists, has set up for himself standards of beauty, which may change from one generation to another, but which represent an aspiration to certain perceived forms from which we attempt to extract a single concept of beauty. This means that we are accepting that there is a concept derived from, but separate from, the works of art which inspire us to believe in the concept. Do we therefore have to put this down as an attribute of the experimenter, who must be believed to have departed to this extent from the minimalism which we have otherwise attributed to him, to include the concept of beauty in the blue-print with which the system of our world constituted itself as one of the consequences of the Big Bang? It seems that it would be perfectly possible to imagine the evolution of the human species taking place with equal success to what has in fact occurred without an aesthetic sense being added to the characteristics of the emerging species. Life would, however, have been very boring, and it is perhaps possible to regard this sense as being a necessary component of a man who can have the power to disregard immediate selfish interests in order to take part in a system of relationships with other human beings which enables the species to maintain its existence.

The aesthetic sense allows man to contemplate something outside the qualities necessary for the practical needs of survival as seen from one famine to the next, and therefore makes it possible for him to have regard to a longer term interest than that involved in getting the better of his neighbour in an ordinary dispute or competition for a source of food, or whatever. The argument may sound a little far-fetched, and it risks introducing value judgements which it has been one of the main purposes of the present enquiry to exclude from the minimalist function of the experimenter. It is rare for different appreciations of the aesthetic to lead to fatal quarrels with other members of the species. Admittedly, people have been known to attack each other owing to rival views of works of art, as has occasionally occurred on the first performances of operas or pieces of music and at the exhibition of novel works of art. And, of course, people have been thought to be guilty of acting against the interests of the state or the majority in propagating novel forms of artistic expression. Nevertheless, the existence of a concept of beauty and the aspirations of people to attain it may on the whole – and with a certain degree of optimism – be regarded as contributing to the process of civilisation and therefore to the better prospects of people being able to live in harmony with each other. By this rather roundabout claim of reasoning, it may therefore be possible to hold that the aesthetic sense was necessary in order to bring about the origination of beings like us, and to give us a reasonable chance of surviving. It could equally, or additionally, be held that the existence of the aesthetic spirit is also consistent with the rather whimsical character of the experimenter which we have seemed to deduce from other aspects of the universe.

Chapter 6

Other Universes

There is a group of theories which suggest that our universe is not the only one, and that others could exist, or do exist already, or may have existed in the past. If any such theories are correct, this could profoundly affect the way in which we build a myth to explain how and why we are here. The simplest version is to suggest that, after the ending of this universe which we have attempted to say must be expected to happen at some distant future date, there could be another universe come into existence, either as a result of a more or less cyclical process, by which universes may end in a Big Crunch and then start again with a new Big Bang, or that a new universe may be started up by the decision of the entity we have called 'The Experimenter' .This would assume that he was dissatisfied with the performance of our existing universe, and wanted to have another try, perhaps with the rules somewhat different in order to produce a different result. If this happened, there would be no trace left of our existence here, unless we are right in thinking that there is a non-material element inherent in, or attached to, us which may be able to continue in non-material surroundings. If that was so, we might then, as suggested earlier, have the curious situation that if there was a similar non-material element in the new universe this, and the one resulting from our experience, might co-exist and therefore presumably be able to communicate one with another. It is curious, if this is so and if there have been other universes in the past that we have, so far as I know, never been given any clue to the existence of such spiritual element belonging to a past universe in all the alleged communications which have been received here by us from the so-called spirit world. It is only too apparent that this kind of hypothesis is clouded in 'ifs' which makes it very difficult to suggest definite conclusions. On the other hand, the general idea of a succession of universes sits quite well with our speculation naming the originator of this process as 'The Experimenter'. It does not, however, get much closer to any idea of who he may be and how he originated – but that is the nature of myths. After a certain point you must not ask too many questions.

Another more radical version of the multiple universe idea is that other universes may exist at the same time as ours. This is a difficult concept to get into one's mind because of our limited appreciation of the space and time in which we live and which appear to take up all the space and time which there is. Other concurrent universes would have to exist in another space and another time which have no means of communication with ours. They are impermeable to any signals we may send, and do not send out any signals that we can receive. There is equally no means of knowing whether they would have the same duration as our universe. If the rules were significantly different from those governing our universe, one could imagine that the duration was very much longer or even, that one or more of them might attain infinite duration, and thus get over the difficulty which we have felt earlier about the paradox of a timeless being creating a time-bound system. In this respect ours could be regarded as a failed experiment, which might, however, have led by a process of analysis to the origination of a better designed system in this respect.

The possibility of some such system of the concurrent multiplicity of universes is to some extent supported by one of the theories relating to the sub-atomic properties of matter and light. As part of the indeterminacy principle, it is suggested that electrons exist in their wave mode until they are perceived and measured by outside interference, whereupon they adopt their particle mode instead. This derives from the view laid down by the principle that you cannot accurately measure the position and speed of a particle or wave because the very act of observing it changes the nature of what you are trying to measure. The happening at the moment of observation is described as the collapse of the wave function. But, assuming that the act of observation is more or less random, there is just as good a chance of the wave not being disturbed at that moment and therefore continuing until something else happens to it. The next point in the theory is that the transformation of the wave into a particle has an effect on everything else that happens in the world, since any event is held to influence every other multiple event. This is the same as the chaos theory example of the butterfly flapping its wings over New York and thereby causing a tornado in the Caribbean. In other words, if it had not flapped its wings, there would not have been a tornado. So the whole picture and history of the universe would have been different if we had not made the observation of the wave at that particular moment. Therefore, there could well be a whole other universe representing the situation in which we had not made the observation. We would not know about this because we only know about the one in which we made the observation. It is, of course, equally unknowable whether the other universe deriving from our absence of observations would be similar to ours or would go off in other directions owing to other random facts of this particular non-action.

The existence of other contemporary universes does not in itself throw any particular new light on the question of our own survival. But it would perhaps be salutary to some notions of the natural superiority of ourselves and our world to think that there might be others going on at the same time which for all we know might be at least as good or better than ours. It might also serve to amplify our picture of the experimenter if we were to think of him as dealing with a multiplicity of universes going on at the same time and not just our own. If we were to believe in some such doctrine as this, there would be an argument in favour of using up some of our research resources in order to try to find a way to make such universes inter-penetrable, and it would give us a more just appreciation of the reality of the world.

Another version of the multiple universe theory could perhaps be derived even more radically from the idealistic philosophy initiated by Berkeley in the 18th century. These views may be summarised by saying that 'everything is in the mind', which is the only reality. What we think of as the outside world is in fact only the projection of ideas inside our mind. Dr Johnson notably thought that he had refuted this theory when he kicked a stone, proving at least to himself that there was a reality out there with which he could directly interact. The theory is also neatly encapsulated in the two limericks:

The first attributed to R.A. Knox:

There was once a man who said 'God'
Must think it exceedingly odd;
If he finds that this tree
Continues to be
When there's no one about in the quad'

Followed by the later rejoinder:

Dear Sir, your astonishment's odd
I am always about in the quad
And that's why the tree
Will continue to be
Since observed by, yours faithfully, God

Continuing in the literary vein, Berkeley's ideas also provided the denouement of the delightful romp through philosophy entitled *Sophie's World*, with the implicit suggestion that the ideas formed in somebody's mind which have an appearance of reality but in fact remained ideas, could nevertheless have a certain tenuous autonomy of their own. On this theory it is possible for anyone to build his own universe as he goes along. The theory will seem to many people to be weird. It represented an attempt to get over the difficult dichotomy of mind and matter and the problem of how they could interact with each other. In this case, mind was supreme and matter could hardly be said to exist without a mind to think it. This is at the other pole from the materialistic view that mind is more or less another name for brain, and represents the impressions that we get from physical processes that go on according to the normal physiological rules.

It is, of course, true that we do not directly apprehend reality or matter. We apprehend the sense-data which seem to emanate from it and by the gradual training of our mind are taken to represent material objects by our minds. So far as the non-material components of human beings – spirit, soul etc. – continues to survive after the death of the material person and existed in a non-material world, then it might be more correct to say that there was nothing but the non-material elements in existence and that there were no material objects there to generate sense-data. In the end, Berkeley might be giving us a description of the spirit world rather than the physical world in which we exist for the time being. The ordinary picture of survival suggests that while we are living in the material world we consist of elements both of material and of non-material character. When the bodily person dies, then if anything is left it can only be the non-material part. And that part would no longer be able to communicate by material means.

The upshot may be that the idea that we create our own universes as we go along may not be very relevant to our enquiry about how the whole thing originated and how it will end. It may, however, give some clues to the nature of a non-material after-life if we wish to believe that such a thing exists. In order to do this we would need to develop the non-material elements which may exist already, but which are at present of a rather fragmentary and inconclusive character. The shift in research required to follow up these thoughts is discussed in a later chapter.

Chapter 7

Morality

Let us at least be clear of one thing. Even if we have to imagine an outside intervention to press the button and make the rules by which our system is going to evolve, we need not add moral principles to this intervention. It is an entirely gratuitous addition to think that the entities we imagine have to be devoted to some moral principles or other.

The importation of morality into the system has to be resisted for two main reasons. One is the inextricable philosophical confusion to which it leads, the other is the exclusivity to which it gives rise and the consequent strife between those who espouse varying moral principles. As regards the confusion, we are faced with the attempt to define good and evil, and to provide for their existence in a system in which it would normally be held that one has to overwhelm the other. It is a little bit like the question of matter and anti-matter in the beginning of the universe. It was owing to the comparatively small preponderance of matter over antimatter in the stages immediately succeeding the Big Bang that produced the universe as we know it. Moralists of a conventional type would no doubt claim that there is a similar preponderance of good over bad by which we are or should be governed, but there is no theoretical reason why this should be the case, and religions have struggled endlessly with the problem. Sometimes the competing principles are personalised as in Zoroaster and Ahuramazda, or, in the Christian version, God and the Devil. You are supposed to believe that one of each of these pairs is better than the other, largely for the reason that this is how he is labelled. Other versions have the non-material world as the state to which we should aspire and the material world, the creation of a more or less wicked demiurge. Here again it does not appear that there is any demonstrable reason why one should be better than the other. You are expected to accept this as a given principle. The problem presents itself in a particularly acute form in more conventional brands of Christianity in which the personalised devil has been relegated to the background and does not appear in polite conversation. Without him you have the apparently insoluble problem of a God who is defined both as omnipotent and as universally good and caring, and yet, as everyone knows, the most terrible things happen, often for no apparent reason, like accidents or wars or plagues, and it is virtually impossible to reconcile omnipotence and benevolence on the one hand and the existence of such manifest evils on the other. As regards exclusivity, it is a sad fact that practically all religions have resulted in the formation of groups of people who held the belief that they are right and that others are wrong. They call themselves orthodox and the others heterodox, or believers against heretics.

Moreover, in many historical cases continuing in some places even today, the consequence of this belief has been that they regard it as their duty to resist the others or convert them by force, or at least carry out propaganda against them. Unfortunately the monotheistic religions seem to have been the greatest offenders in this respect. The Old Testament is full of stories of Jews killing non-Jews because they did not accept the Jewish religion. The Christians persecuted heretics from a very early date, seeing it as their duty either to forcibly convert or to exterminate non-believers. One of the Byzantine emperors was described to me by a Greek Orthodox priest in the Sinai monastery in the following terms: 'He was a great Christian: he killed many heathens'. The wars of religions between two sects of the Christian religion devastated Europe in the 17th century and the difference between these two sects has continued to divide Northern Ireland until now, with numerous fatal results on both sides. The Jews in Europe were exterminated by a supposedly Christian country, simply because of their religion. Muslims actually divided the world into the spheres of the believers and non-believers, and thought it their duty to conquer the latter. (It must be recorded, however, that in later years the Muslims were capable of showing far more tolerance of persecuted minorities than their Christian neighbours, as witnessed by the reception in the Ottoman Empire of the Jews who were expelled from Spain and Portugal at the end of the 15th century). The tragic recent history of Palestine has been due to the dogmatic beliefs of Muslims and Jews about the righteousness of their cause set against the followers of the other religion. In the debate which followed the Spanish occupation of Latin America, a great part of the justification of this action was found to be in the opportunity it gave to bring hundreds of thousands, or millions, of pagan inhabitants into the fold of the Catholic church. And in the course of this exercise, the native culture was, so far as was possible, destroyed. The partition of India in 1947 was brought about because of the intransigent religious beliefs of Hindus and Muslims and the impossibility of reconciling them in a single state. The total numbers of people killed in these conflicts based on religion must be far greater than those in nationalistic or dynastic wars.

I insist on the harmful effects of religious belief because the easiest answer to some of the metaphysical questions which I have posed has often seemed to be to assume that there is a God to direct the physical world, and the spiritual world even more, and that his power and its everlasting duration can provide the answers to the questions of what went before and what comes after. In fact, the penalties for such beliefs have almost always been that the people who have them consider themselves exclusive against those who do not and believe it is their duty either to convert or exterminate the heathens. What I am trying to explore is the possibility of a system which has produced the world as we know it, but does not necessarily bring the terrible consequences that belief in God has almost always brought in the past. Our job, on the contrary, is to go so far as we possibly can in the direction of finding explanations for these difficult questions without having recourse to a supernatural being, at least of the kind which seems to impose rigidity and exclusivity of belief on its adherents. The idea of a rather indifferent and bored experimenter seems to meet the requirement adequately, without having these effects, and leaving morality to be deduced from the common sense way of behaving towards our fellow creatures in ways that promote the general welfare, including our own satisfaction.

It is impossible at this remote distance to say whether the battles of pre-historic men with each other originated from the sense of territory or hunting ground or agricultural settlements and were given a religious basis by the invention on each side of gods who were supposed to add to their strength by opposing the gods of the other side, or whether the original communities had come to believe in some supernatural entities to explain the natural phenomena which they could not otherwise understand, and were inspired by these beliefs to oppose others with whom they came into contact, and whose gods were somehow different. Nor can we say that it was a natural characteristic of man to follow his instinct in a belligerent way from the beginning, and whether this was a natural and necessary part of evolution, but we can, without question, say that the religious element which either existed from the beginning or was imported for other reasons gravely exacerbated the conflicts and made them less easy to solve. In seeking a minimalist myth to explain our existence, there is no need to repeat these mistakes and to imagine that whoever pushed the switch to start everything off had moral purposes in view which he bequeathed to us as the ultimate product of the Big Bang.

It is perfectly possible to deduce an acceptable system of moral behaviour simply from a consideration of the relations of human beings to each other, and the ways in which these relations can be made more generally acceptable and enjoyable. Hobbes imagined that the nasty, short and brutish existence of our ancestors was changed by the acceptance of a social contract which bound them to behave to each other in a way that did not lead to conflict or the oppression of one by the other. It is indeed remarkable that the belief in humanism should have survived for many hundreds of years of religious bigotry and oppression and the thousands of years during which tyrannical gods have been invented by equally tyrannical men and their opponents persecuted. But the existence of humanism today and the general decline in religious observance and dogmatism, at any rate in the west, hopefully justifies us in regarding the prevalence of exclusive religions as an aberration in the history of mankind from from which we now have the opportunity to escape. It also justifies us in believing that the origination of the world was morally neutral and was not inspired by some great design of a religious nature as a means of imposing morality, and securing the victory of good over evil.

In addition to the wars between states and within states, and the persecution of those of another state to which religion has given grounds, it has also had many harmful social effects. It has issued precepts based on magic, superstition, beliefs in supernatural forces, and the domination of a priestly class over the rest of the population to enforce harmful practices of various kinds. The general subordination of women is one example; others are the attempts to prevent the use of birth control which has immeasurably added to the problems of excessive population in various parts of the world, the forbidding of divorce and abortion, the forbidding of various kinds of food. This may in some cases have had a hygienic origin, but has been used as a distinguishing mark of one creed against another. Its social effect is silly rather than harmful, but nevertheless it is typical of the recourse to authority, usually of a supernatural kind, instead of reason, which characterises the exercise of religious power through the ages. Another example is the horrible procedure of female circumcision, still practised over large areas of Africa and Asia. This may perhaps not have been strictly religious in origin, but it is the forces of religion which impede the attempt made in a few countries to abolish the practice.

These reflections on the evils that have too often followed the belief of religious people in the supernatural sanction of morality need to be completed by a fuller description of the alternative which has been provided by the history and prospects of humanism.

Humanism was first recognised as a literary, intellectual and aesthetic movement in the 15th Century in Italy, to some extent outside the Church, but also seeking to influence it from within. After a period of toleration, both the Reformation and the counter-reformation were hostile to it because of its insistence on the free will of the individual. But it came back with renewed strength in the age of enlightenment and thus contributed in a big way to both the American and French Revolutions. Later on, though the name was not so much used, it provided the Mediterranean-classical input to the romantic movement and at the same time was identified on the scientific side of the argument that raged through so much of the later part of the 19th Century between the theories of Darwin and Huxley on the one hand and the Church on the other.

Historically, humanism's first job was to get rid of the clutter and obscurity of the Middle Ages, to re-discover the clarity and autonomy of the classical worlds which had preceded them. The. renaissance could hardly have happened without humanism. Renaissance means rebirth – but of what? The Italian scholars of the 15th Century re-discovered antiquity in the manuscripts of classical authors hitherto largely hidden in the monasteries, and in the architecture which fortunately was still lying about on the surface of the Italian landscape. There arrived from these discoveries three vital ingredients of the culture of succeeding ages: firstly, the pagan subjects of art to which we owe the masterpieces of Botticelli and others, the rebirth of realistic sculpture as in Donatello and the classical architecture of Brunelleschi, Palladio, and Wren. Secondly, the rigorous methods of classical scholarship which largely changed the nature of intellectual discourse. Thirdly, and most importantly, a view of the position of man in the world in relation to the presence or absence of supernatural beings. The classical world was largely sceptical of the religion which it had inherited from earlier ages. The behaviour of the gods and goddesses was the behaviour of fallible men and women writ large; unjust and inhumane results flowed from superstitious adherence to primitive belief in the vagaries of the gods of Olympus. Lucretius, the Latin poet of the lst Century BC, after describing the sacrifice by Agamemnon of his daughter in order to secure a favourable wind for the Greek fleet to proceed to Troy, wrote, 'Religion was capable of producing so much evil'. The more sophisticated morality of people like Cicero and Seneca was derived from the Stoic school of philosophy, which had no place for divine intervention but emphasised the responsibility of the individual to make the best of the world in which he finds himself.

It is remarkable that the humanists were able to get away so easily with their pursuance of classical models irrespective of whether these were compatible with the dogmas of the Catholic church. This was partly because during the 15th Century the Papacy was only just recovering from the schism which had led to rival Popes being established in France and in Italy, and was therefore still comparatively weak. But more than this, such cohabitation between the Classical and the Christian was not altogether new. As early as a hundred years before, for example, Dante was accompanied during his poetic visit to the Inferno and the Purgatorio not by a Christian guide but by the Roman poet Virgil. Only when he gets to the Paradiso can he no longer be accompanied by Virgil since the latter did not have the advantage of a Christian upbringing. On the other hand, even at the beginning of the Paradiso, Dante makes an invocation, not to a Christian saint or teacher, but to the pagan god Apollo. Moreover, the church had for a long time adopted as its own quite a large amount of the teachings of the Greek philosopher Aristotle. So the boundary was already rather fuzzy. It was thus possible for one of the leading humanists to say in the mid-15th Century that much was to be learned from Augustine, but to understand moral problems it was essential to grapple with the ideas of Epicurus, Zeno and Aristotle; and Cosimo de'Medici said about the same time that he recognised in platonic philosophy the fairest flower of the ancient world of thought, and that without Plato it would be hard to be a good Christian. A rather more comic example is that in the general fever to obtain relics of saints etc. as objects of prestige for churches and cathedrals, the King of Naples obtained from Venice a leg bone of the Roman historian Livy and received it with ceremony on its entrance into his City.

The Dutch scholar Erasmus had no difficulty in accepting the appellation of humanist while remaining a Catholic priest all his life. Erasmus introduced the study of Greek to Cambridge University where, in the early years of the 16th Century, he was professor of both Greek and Divinity. Erasmus, and to some extent the humanists generally contributed to the origins of the reformation by calling attention to the unworthiness and corruption of the Catholic clergy but, after correspondence with the originators of the reformation who wanted to claim him as one of them, Erasmus refused to participate, largely on account of the reformation introducing an equally dogmatic approach to religion as that to which he objected in the Catholic church. Erasmus' great friend, Sir Thomas More, was also known as a Christian humanist, partly because of his composition in Latin of *Utopia*, but more because he shared Erasmus' view on the desirability of a more rational theology and for radical reform in the clergy. He, as is well known, paid with his life for his continuing devotion to the Primacy of Rome.

Before moving on from the renaissance, we have to note with regret that, while the humanists claimed to derive a satisfactory system of morality from the ancient philosophers, they did not use the doctrine of humanism as encompassing the whole human race. The city states of Italy, for whom the humanists worked as administrators and propagandists, did not cease from fighting each other. This is a missed potential of humanism which, even now, has not been adequately developed.

The cosy relationship of the humanists with the church could not last indefinitely. Luther nailed his thesis to the church door at Wittenberg in 1517. The Reformation led inevitably to the counter-reformation, which entailed the clamping down of the hatches by the Papacy in all directions. While humanism was not directly involved with the reformation, nevertheless it was submerged in the wave of orthodoxy and repression now emanating from the Vatican.

The humanists, as well as the reformers, had been belabouring the institutions of the church for the corrupt and materialistic way in which the clerics behaved (over the sale of indulgences etc.).

After the struggles of the reformation had begun, it was no longer possible for the church to listen to such accusations without trying to stop their circulation and punish those who originated them. By the end of the 16th Century, the rigours of the counter-reformation had extended also to science, which had flourished in the humanist environment. In 1616, Galileo, the great Italian astronomer, had to promise to the Vatican to abstain from advocating the system he had inherited from Copernicus, that is to say, that the earth revolves round the sun rather than the other way round. And in 1632, when he published another work in favour of this system, he was put in prison by the Inquisition.

But the re-imposition of obscurantism also could not last. In the very year that Galileo died, Newton was born and the relations of science to religion would never be the same again. The poet Alexander Pope, who inherited much of the mantle of the humanists, encapsulated the change in his famous epigram 'Nature and Nature's laws lay hid in night: God said "Let Newton be and all was light".' (Although it is almost entirely irrelevant to our subject, I cannot forebear to quote the rejoinder to these lines written by J. C. Squire two hundred and fifty years later: 'It did not last: the devil howling "Ho! Let Einstein be" restored the status quo')

Pope has the further merit of expressing more explicitly and more poetically than before the system of morality which can be derived simply from man's situation in this world. In his great poem *The Essay on Man* he urges that mankind should not strive to reach above itself: 'Know then thyself, presume not God to scan. The proper study of mankind is man'. And he goes on to claim that a proper balance between the human characteristics of passion and reason can provide a sufficient basis for the virtuous conduct of man, including respect for, and care for, his fellow men, and concludes, 'That reason, passion, answer one great aim; that true self-love and social are the same: that virtue only makes out this below and all our knowledge is, ourselves to know'. Later in the 18th Century, a similar view was put forward by an eminent churchman, Bishop Berkeley, who said that a satisfactory system of morality could be based on what he called 'cool self-love'. In other words, as we might put it now, we are endowed by nature with a gregarious instinct and we gain satisfaction in indulging it and doing good to our fellow men, recognising that we are all part of the human family.

Humanism can claim a good deal of the parentage of the age of enlightenment in the 18th Century. The debates of the philosophers about morality, society and politics were based on the unwritten assumption that the answers to these questions were to be found in the nature of man and in the system of education which should be applied to human beings to make them better members of society. Pope proved to have been optimistic in proposing a proper balance between passion and reason as the only solution required. The Scottish philosopher Hume restated the question 'concerning the general foundation of morals; whether they be derived from reason, or from sentiment; whether we attain the knowledge of them by a chain of argument and induction, or by an immediate feeling and finer internal sense'. Rousseau idealised the latter by his advocacy of the state of nature as a principal source of good. The primacy of reason as propounded by Diderot and his fellow encyclopaedists culminated in the enthronement of an actress as the representation of reason in Notre-Dame by the French revolutionaries. Before this, the Declaration of Independence of the United States in 1776 stated: 'We hold these truths to be self evident, that all men are created equal, that they are endowed by their creator with certain inalienable rights, that among these are life, liberty and the pursuit of happiness'. The power and responsibility of human beings to decide their own future was emphasised in the first federalist paper by Alexander Hamilton in 1783: 'It seems to have been reserved to the people of this country to decide the important question, whether societies of men are really capable or not of establishing good government'. Another humanist characteristic was that the founders of the American Republic insisted on the separation of Church and State, echoing the remark of the historian Gibbon: 'The philosophers of Greece deduced their morals from the nature of man rather than from that of God'.

Before we become too euphoric it has to be recalled that humanist principles did not prevent the barbarous treatment by the Americans of the American Indians, or of the immigrant Negroes initially as slaves, or later as allegedly equal members of society. Equally, we have to face the question whether the excesses of the French Revolution, culminating in the Terror, were a consequence of the enthronement of reason or if not, what went wrong.

If humanism can take a lot of the credit for the principles of the American Revolution and the subsequent constitution of the United States, must it also take some of the blame for what happened in the later stages of the French Revolution? The principles on which this revolution began: 'Liberty, Equality, Fraternity', are good humanist principles and the undermining of the authority of the church and of an autocratic government which preceded the revolution were also in the humanist tradition.

What went wrong can be well epitomised in the story of Madame Roland, wife of a minister in one of the earlier revolutionary governments, but who subsequently ended up on the scaffold. She 'prided herself on a positively Roman virtue', was 'steeped in the theories of Rousseau and, like so many of her contemporaries a passionate admirer of the Greek and Roman past'. After a fervent catholic childhood, she had rejected the doctrines of the Church. But when the moderate revolutionary faction which she had supported was overturned by the Jacobins she was unable to change her principles and join the extremists and paid for this with her life, exclaiming on the scaffold 'O Liberty, what crimes are committed in thy name'. Charlotte Corday, who had also grown up steeped in the lofty ideals of Greek and Roman history, was inspired by some of the more extreme incidents of that history to put her ideas into violent action, and assassinated the revolutionary leader Marat in his bath.

Humanism cannot guarantee, any more than any other doctrine, to prevent the excesses of passion, or of reason, and there can be no doubt that the French Revolution, in spite of its high ideals put back by its excesses the development of individual liberty in western Europe for a considerable time. The immediate response was the establishment of autocracy in France under Napoleon, and after his collapse, the establishment of a generally autocratic policy among the states of Western Europe still fearful that the revolutionary seeds might spread from France to other countries. On the continent, this took the form of the League of the Three Emperors (Russia, Prussia and Austria), united in repressing further revolutions as in 1848, and in England the repressive laws and heavy penalties of the post-Napoleonic era, paradoxically coupled with the birth of the evangelical Christian movement, which, as Wilberforce himself admitted, could be seen as an instrument of stability. 'Christianity,' he said, 'renders the inequalities of the social state less galling to the lower orders, whom also She instructs, in their turn, to be diligent, humble, patient; reminding them that their more lowly path has been allotted to them by the hand of God; that it is their part faithfully to discharge its duties and contentedly to bear its inconveniences . . .'

With these set-backs to its political mission, humanism becomes prominent again in the 19th Century as part of the inspiration of the romantics in literature. Keats rediscovered for himself the 'classical world' – "On first looking into Chapman's Homer" – and used

Greek pastoral poetry as a model for his 'Ode on a Grecian Urn'. Shelley said, 'We are all Greeks' and adopted the principle of individual freedom and the individual human consciousness as the source of man's knowledge of truth and morality. Later in the century, George Eliot, the most philosophical of the Victorian novelists, restated the humanist philosophy by saying, 'Fellowship between man and man has been the principle of social and moral development and is not dependent on the conception of what is not man, and the idea of God is the ideal of a goodness entirely human; in other words, an exaltation of the human'. Later still, William Ernest Henley struck a more dramatic humanist note: 'I thank whatever gods may be for my unconquerable soul . . . It matters not how strait the gate, how charged with punishments the scroll, I am the master of my Fate, I am the captain of my soul.'

It is deeply shocking to humanists that churches who have claimed to have supernatural authority for the moral teachings which they propound should have behaved with such terrible cruelty. In the Crusades, for example, the Christians behaved with much greater ferocity and ruthlessness than the Moslems. The capture of Jerusalem by the Christians in 1099 was followed by the massacre of the Jewish and Moslem inhabitants. When Saladin re-conquered it 100 years later, the Frankish Christians were allowed to leave and the Orthodox to go on living there. The word 'Crusader' was until recently used as a term of abuse in Turkish politics, in the sense of vandal or hooligan. The 'Catholic Kings' of Spain, having completed the re-conquest of their country from the Arabs, expelled the large Jewish population from Spain, simply on the grounds that they would not whole-heartedly accept Christianity. The refugee Jews were hospitably received by the Ottoman Empire, and this gave rise to the flourishing Sephardic communities throughout the Eastern Mediterranean. Worse still, the Christians were equally barbarous against each other. The

Cathars were a peaceable group of people practising their own version of Christianity, whose influence spread through much of southern France in the 12th century. Because they would not accept the orthodox variety of Catholicism, they were liquidated in a so-called crusade sponsored by the King of France and the Vatican, and the Inquisition was set up by the Dominican friars to extirpate the last remnants of their heresy. After the Reformation, western Europe was plagued by wars of religion throughout the 16th and 17th centuries, and here in England ecclesiastics of one variety or another were in turn burnt at the stake according to the religious adherence of successive monarchs.

It is hardly an exaggeration to say that the slogan was 'my version of God is better than yours, therefore I am going to exterminate you,' sometimes adding: 'for the good of your immortal soul.' Much of the same injustice contributed to Imperialism. The Teutonic knights invaded Lithuania not only to acquire territory but also to bring the benefit of Christianity to the Pagan Lithuanians (and, incidentally to forestall their being converted to Orthodox Christianity by the Russians). It was one of the principal motives of the Spanish conquest of central and southern America that they hoped, by these means, to add adherents to the Catholic Faith. And there were dreadful hypocritical debates on whether it was right to enslave the natives because they were not Christian. The religious wars in Western Europe more or less died out during the 18th Century, but were replaced only too easily by dynastic politics and national advantage as motives for wars which continued without abatement. But even here the religious elements in war did not disappear altogether. Sometimes the two were mixed together, and divine support was claimed for whatever national or dynastic cause was at stake, as for example the Divine Right of Kings, the British Royal motto *Dieu et mon droit*, Henry V's cry before Harfleur, 'God for England, Harry and St. George' and the notorious episode of the 'Angels of Mons' in the First World War when supernatural powers were claimed to have supported the allied operations. It would not surprise me if the Germans claimed that another lot of angels were supporting them. The story is in the same tradition as Homer's description in the *Iliad* of gods and goddesses intervening to protect their favourite heroes on either side in the Trojan war.

Finally, what is the relevance of humanism in the sea of troubles with which we are faced today? It is, I think, twofold. First it can continue to hold up the light of reason against the dogma claiming supernatural origins which inspires fundamentalism in more than one religion. The one with which we are most familiar is, of course, that of Islam. One of the problems of Islam is that it did not have a humanistic movement recalling it to the man-based standard of an earlier classical age, nor indeed did it have a reformation. It is in many respects still living in its own middle ages. The methods of justice and the scale of punishment inflicted by the Moslem religious code belong to an era which we consider barbaric. There is also still the concentration on the minutiae of doctrine which we find so reminiscent of the debates of the school-men of our Middle Ages.

Unfortunately, Islam is not the only religion to have a fundamentalist element within it. The so-called Bible belt in America was once almost laughable in opposing the teaching of evolution in its schools. It has now transformed itself into something more sinister called the 'religious right', which seems to be becoming a factor of some importance in Republican politics in America. In its more extreme form, it too would seek to impose its ideas on communities and on individuals as demonstrated by actual physical actions taken against abortion clinics and those who practice in them. What is so lacking here, as in the other cases I have mentioned, is the tolerance derived from the feeling of community with the human race and not merely the blind adherence to one sub-group of it.

One of the characters in a play by Terence, a Latin playwright of the 2nd century BC, says, '*Homo sum: humani nil a me alienum puto*' – 'I am a man, I count nothing human foreign to me'. Echoed by John Donne some 1800 years later in his resounding lines, 'No man is an island, entire of itself . . . any man's death diminishes me, because I am involved in mankind; and therefore never send to know for whom the bell tolls; it tolls for thee'. These sentiments have never been given the resonance that they deserve in the conduct of international relations or between competing social groups. The general feeling that one is part of humanity has been superseded almost continuously by the competing claims of belonging to a smaller group united by ties of superstition, dogma, tribal loyalty and so on. However lofty the sentiments with which a group is formed, and I include most of the world's religions, its almost immediate effect is to separate off this group from the rest, to give it a feeling of exclusivity and discrimination and superiority. 'My god is better than your god. Therefore I have a duty to convert you or exterminate you'. 'My tribe is stronger than yours, therefore you have to submit to me'. Hence wars of religion, tribal wars, class prejudice, racial prejudice, colour prejudice etc., etc. It may be that in man's long pre-history it seemed necessary to stick together in groups of family and tribe for self protection, or the defence of hunting grounds. Must this imprint such a strong instinct on succeeding generations and make it impossible to get away from particularism and remember the claims of humanity as a whole?

Humanism does not guarantee any more than Christianity, or any other religion, that there will not be wickedness or that humans will not have to combine to resist it when it impinges on human values. The resistance can be stronger if it is in the name of common humanity not of another race or religion or nation or tribe. Humanity or humaneness is the criterion by which one can judge, the highest quality to which an appeal can be made. The people on both sides of a quarrel are men and women before they are protestant or catholic, orthodox or moslem, Bosnians or Serbs, Armenians or Azerbaijanis.

The reconciliation of diversity with the over-riding obligation to behave as members of the human race is a vital part of the humanist agenda, and of the survival agenda.

I have made this rather lengthy excursion into the history and philosophy of humanism because to many people its nature is not familiar, and because it is vital to the argument of this enquiry that there should be seen to be a viable alternative to the claims of religions and dogma, whose consequences are so often damaging. In contemplating even a temporary myth we are entering dangerous ground, because myths have so often given rise to exclusivity and sectarianism, and it is important to realise that there is a basis for good behaviour between members of the human race which does not derive from a supernatural sanction.

Chapter 8

The Direction of Research

If the dispersal of the galaxies and the intricacies of the sub-atomic structure of matter are merely incidental and perhaps even accidental features of the main purposes with which the universe was created, the question may be asked, whether the amount of research carried out into these areas is well directed. We are often told, of course, that the pure research into the nature of the world for its own sake is the highest occupation of the scientist, and that, in addition, to the rewards of this kind of study in themselves there are frequently spin-offs which have practical application and improve the quality of life. This may be so, but pure research may also, at some times, be a luxury that we can ill afford. It may be time that we consider again the ultimate purpose of the limited degree of scientific research which it will be possible to carry out at any one time owing to the shortage of resources, both human and material. Although it may seem that we have a comfortable cushion of many millions of years before either the death of the sun or the death of the universe, nevertheless the transformations to give us, or our descendents, any hope of prolonging an existence of some kind beyond these catastrophes are so great that it would be desirable to begin taking these objectives in mind more seriously.

In order to survive the death of the sun, we, or some of us, have to go somewhere else, either in our own galaxy or another galaxy. This means that we have to vastly increase our knowledge of other possible sites for habitation. To do this we have to discover whether there are any other intelligent beings who might be able to provide information which would help us in this task, or whose existence might, at any rate, indicate areas to which we should pay particular attention in looking for another site. The difficulties and slowness of communicating with other beings in a different part of the universe are so great that we should give particular attention to the improvement of our interstellar communication, especially the possibility of conducting it at speeds greater than that of light. We then have to give a great deal of attention to improving the means of travel for our own descendants to another site once we have found it, and to the means of making it habitable. On the present basis of knowledge, this would include the design of spaceships in which people could live for more than one generation, and the means of propulsion for such vehicles. In order to prepare for the conversion of an alien environment into one which will permit human existence, we could well practise on say, Mars, in order to overcome the apparent absence of air and water on that planet which renders it uninhabitable, unless a large degree of transformation is brought about.

One of the beauties of setting research targets of this kind will be that the effort will inevitably have to be international on a grand scale, because otherwise the total resources will not be adequate and because, if there is any quarrelling between the nations or groups of nations, this will dissipate resources that will be needed for the common purpose. The institutional framework will, of course, have to be decided. Can it, for example, be done without world government? This would terrify many people, but has many attractions of its own. There would be no need to take this decision immediately, but a sufficiently strong scientific framework would have to be installed from the beginning. CERN – The European Council for Organisations for Nuclear Research – plus America, Russia and China would be the obvious components to begin with. Others might be added if they were able and willing to provide resources either of an intellectual or material kind. Universality will have to be avoided, which would be a blow to some idealists, and the use of United Nations machinery would therefore have to be avoided at all costs. One of the major problems, of course, would be that simple and perhaps rather brutal propositions of this kind would not be acceptable to a larger number of well disposed people, unless and until the danger was more apparent and imminent. But the enormous time lag to produce any results makes it necessary to consider how to start moving towards them, even when this is not the case and when it is only too easy to say, 'Oh well, we have X million or billion years, so there's no need to do anything unpleasant for the time being'.

When we finally approach the situation when travel to another site might be contemplated, there would be the other enormous question of who was to take part in the travel and, first of all, whether it would be necessary to bring about an artificial evolution of part of the human race in a direction that might make it more likely to survive at whatever site for its future might be chosen. And, if so, how many generations would this take? Perhaps the time is not as long as all that. It would be endlessly fascinating to consider what should be the criteria for selecting our future space travellers. Should they be average, should they be supermen and superwomen? Should they be especially equipped with knowledge and practice of various disciplines and skills and physical characteristics? Should they all be educated in how to get on with each other?

So far all this is designed to prolong the existence of the human species within the present material universe. This would allow its existence to be a great deal longer than that of our present solar system, but it would not serve the purpose when we finally ran out of suns to which we could attach ourselves. In order to do this, we would need to rely on the non-material elements which may exist already but which are at present of a rather fragmentary and inconclusive type. One of the ways to approach the development of this part of the subject would be to increase, by a very large factor, the amount of resources directed to research into such topics as psychical phenomena, including telepathy, extra-sensory perception, telekinesis, or the ability to influence material by non-material means. The present scientific approach to phenomena of this kind is most unsatisfactory. The great majority of established scientists refuse to take psychical research seriously or to accept even the best evidenced events within this sphere, because to do so would mean that the scientific rules – by which they have spent their lives and their intellectual experience – would be found to be either wrong or incomplete and the rules applying to these phenomena would seem at first sight to transgress many of the maxims of scientific law. Moreover, the experimentation is extremely difficult since repeatability is not at present a feature of many psychic phenomena, and the incidence of experimenter effect is unusually high. We are talking about a major shift in the scientific paradigm. The general purpose would be to establish the reality of phenomena which lie outside the normal rules of science, to develop the capability to bring these about, to establish the question of whether the non-material elements which seem to be involved with these phenomena constitute a reality which might be able to survive the absence of a material universe and if so, to partake in the timelessness which appears to be a feature of existence before and after the existence of the material universe.

Another line of enquiry should be about the production of intelligent machines. This would be directed particularly towards exploring the possibility of their autonomy, so that they could continue to exist after the people who had set them up were no longer there. There would also be the search for the possibility of operating such machines on very low energy inputs. The ultimate objective would be to create a machine that could detach itself from the people who created it, perhaps after several generations of evolution generated by the original machine itself, and adopt a position outside the normal limitations of the system inside which it was created. It could then be used, instead of space travel, by individuals to explore the possibilities of localities in which it might be possible for intelligent beings to operate, and would be programmed to create such beings in a suitable place either directly or partly through stages of evolution such as we have experienced. This may sound an impossible task, but we will not know until we have tried. Other lines of research would straddle the gap between pure scientific research into the nature of matter etc., and goal-directed research objectives which we have been discussing. The purpose would be to investigate whether it was possible to escape the two limitations imposed by the theories of relativity. One is that which relates energy inseparably to mass ($E=mc^2$). The other is the limitation of speed to the speed of light. It might seem strange to suggest that the work of Einstein, the great iconoclast, who broke down the previously existing rules of physics and of the nature of the universe, should himself now need some revision. But it would be wrong to suggest that his theories necessarily represent finality any more than those of Newton which he overthrew.

To produce energy we normally carry out a transformation of matter, as for example by burning coal to produce electricity or by drawing directly on the sun's energy to produce light and heat.

The energy coming to us from the sun is produced by the transformation of matter in the sun. But there are certain things which do not seem to depend on energy of this kind, but rather on energy which we cannot at present measure as it carries out its work. Examples are psychical communications and the non-local effects of one photon on another in order to maintain symmetry or other characteristics of the two photons. So far as we can ascertain at present, these kinds of energy are not derived from the transformation of matter as we presently understand. Psychic communication, as in telepathy, appears to take place between the non-material elements of two people. Meaningful information can be transmitted in this way, just as it can be transmitted by the normal means of communication, depending on energy whose course we can trace with instruments. An interesting characteristic of this kind of energy for our present discussion is that its transmission does not seem to depend on the normal processes of space and time, in that distance appears to make no difference to it and there is no measurable time lag between the despatch of the information and its receipt. We seem, therefore, to be faced with the phenomenon of energy which is not derived from matter and which operates outside the normal constraints on our means of communication. If this kind of energy could be harnessed more regularly than is at present the case, this would be of immeasurable importance, both for the facilitation of communications between different parts of the universe and also as promoting the speculation that there is a non-material aspect of the universe which, because of this characteristic, might survive the disappearance of the material universe. The transfer of hitherto non-measurable energy to bring about these phenomena is so difficult that one is forced to consider another view. This is, that the remote participants in either psychic phenomena or non locality cases could be regarded not as separate entities between whom some external means of communication has to be set up, but as parts of wholes so that the links between them are, so to speak, internal and organic. This would mean that, rather than try to detect energy transfers taking place, we would have to study the nature of the wholeness and the meaning of any such term and the nature of the links between different parts of the whole which can allow these means of communication. Hitherto, so little attention has been paid to this kind of concept that the study of it may seem as difficult as that of the attempt to discover new means of energy transfer which seemed to partake of a non-material character. Such ideas are, or could be, related to the idea mentioned above, that on the death of a person in the material world, the non-material element inherent in some way in that person does not have a personal non-material survival, but is joined up with a collective.

The idea of wholeness and oneness has many adherents today, and the similarity between ideas of this kind and those of some eastern religions will be readily apparent. If it were true, this would have important effects on the concept of the myth which we are exploring to account for our origins. If oneness is the dominant mode, it is hard to see how the transition from this situation to the Big Bang could take place, particularly as the most important consequence of the Big Bang, according to the views expressed in the present enquiry, has been to produce strongly individualistic human persons with aspirations to personal fulfilment, intensity of personal relations, and the hope of survival. To accept that there is no personal survival, but that whatever non material elements there may have been attached to the living person, become submerged in death with an amorphic mass of being, would seem to negate the principle of purpose which we are conditioned to ascribe to any action taken by an intelligent being. It is not easy to detect the purpose in a static and amorphous mass, except in the one action which is known to us, namely the creation of the material world through the Big Bang.

One might speculate wildly on an evolutionary framework for the spirit world of oneness. There could be individual survivors who were trying to escape oneness to pursue their differentiated existence in another dimension to that which they had previously existed. This would in some ways mirror the experience of primitive organisms who escaped in the early days of the material world from the primeval swamp and evolved into the organisms that we know in the world today. A scenario like this might perhaps account for the fragmentary and fugitive nature of the communication alleged to be received from the spiritual surviving element of dead human beings. It might also look forward to a continuing evolution of spirits towards a destination which is entirely unknown to us, and perhaps to them. We have come a long way in our mission. It is quite unclear and a matter for personal choice whether our experimenter should be regarded as having set up the oneness and then added the Big Bang as a contrast or with a feeling that the result of the origination of the oneness was far from satisfactory. Or he could be regarded as the original rebel against the pervading oneness, somewhat on the lines of a beneficent Lucifer, (reverting to the original meaning of his name – bright morning star).

The framing of research into these aspects of survival is, of course, exceptionally difficult, and would require the participation of philosophers as well as scientists; perhaps quite a good opportunity to get the two normally antagonistic disciplines to collaborate.

The other enormous difficulty is to get those in power in the world to focus their minds on objectives as far away as the ones we are speaking of. We all know that the average contemplation span for a democratic politician is less than five years – the length of time between elections. It is very hard to think of an election being won on a programme of migration to another solar system in 5 billion years or so. And yet the resources needed to initiate such a programme will inevitably diminish the amounts available for health and social security now. The difficulty is all the greater when we consider how much of the American and Russian space programmes were thought affordable because of nationalistic rivalry rather than communal effort, whereas the resources for research on the lines we are advocating will, of necessity, have to be done on the basis of world cooperation. A change of mind-set may be one of the earlier requirements. Is 6 billion years enough? It depends on when you begin.

Chapter 9

Why Not Start With Us?

One of the many enigmas which we have left unsolved is the nature and characteristics of the being we have called the experimenter. We have suggested two or three things about him (or her), largely negative. His power should be minimalist, that is to say just adequate to bring about the Big Bang and so set in motion the processes which led to the present state of affairs, coupled presumably with some rules by which the material world, and the forces controlling it, should operate and develop. This means that he should not claim to be all-powerful, or to have any moral qualities, or to be able or willing to intervene in the affairs of the world once they have started rolling within the parameters which he has endowed the process with. We have suggested that several aspects of the world, as it has developed, suggest that he may have some whimsical characteristics and that the object, or one of the main objects, of what he has done would be to create circumstances in which we, the only purposeful beings known to us at present in the universe, might be able to exist. It has not been clear why he should have wished to do this. We have held open the strong possibility that our world should be regarded as one of the experiments, not necessarily the only one, and that others might have taken place or others might take place after us. But there is one particular question that has to be addressed, not solely to the experimenter as we are trying to guess what he might be like, but with even greater force to the creative forces of most other religions. The question is: if we are the end products of the developments of the universe since the Big Bang, why was it necessary to go through all the long and painful process of evolution to produce us, with the outcome being very uncertain at various times? If the object was that we should be in existence, why was the effort not directed simply to bringing that about, de novo, rather than going through the difficult processes of the formation of a planet at a certain fixed temperature, humidity, atmosphere etc. and also the laws of evolution which, with many a hiccup, in the end produced creatures like us after innumerable false starts with different kinds of hominid. It was a difficult and doubtful process, which, with the originator being regarded as all-powerful, could have been avoided. We have partly answered this by suggesting that our creator, that is to say, the experimenter, was not all-powerful in the sense used by religions, but executed minimum functions required to get the process going initially. In the earlier versions of monotheistic religions, cosmology provided for an immediate creation of humanity as described in the Book of Genesis. Later commentators even gave a date for this happening – 4004BC. The discovery of evolution and of the fossil record supporting it made this particular myth so unrealistic that it had to be dropped (except in a few States of the United States). There was a rear-guard action which consisted of trying to suggest that the fossils had been created at the same time, and were left in their positions as means of distracting people from the fixed doctrines of the creation, whether by God or the Devil was not always clear. But when the evolutionary story was accepted by most civilised thinkers, even those who followed a religion, not much effort was made to suggest a reason for which the Creator chose to work through the archaeological and anthropological records which were being progressively laid before us in greater detail and cohesion. In a curious way, the story of the Garden of Eden was more logical than the geological record, if it was accepted that the general purpose of creation was that there should ultimately be people in existence like us.

If the object of the coming into being of the world as we know it was not to produce us, what was the object? We can say that the other productions of nature which surround us are very remarkable and, according to our aesthetic sense, in many cases beautiful. This line of thought is getting near to a naive pantheism by which everything in the world would be endowed with a portion of divinity, not only the living things also but sticks and stones as well. There is no need absolutely to exclude ideas of this kind. They would attribute a rather diffuse kind of purposefulness to the creator or our experimenter, rather different from the purposefulness with which we ourselves are endowed. It is quite difficult to see how two such different manifestations of purpose should have participated in the origination of our world. If we try to think of a more coherent purpose for our experimenter, there are a few different options. There would be one which might seem unduly cynical. This would envisage the experimenter saying, presumably to himself, 'Let's have a go. Press the button and see what happens.'

Within the unknowingness of our origins in which we now stand, it is equally permissible to think that we are one in a series of universes, a series of experiments, of which some earlier versions have failed, failed that is even in producing beings as rational as ourselves. The margins of survival have been narrow. The temperature had to be just right within a few degrees; the mix of chemical elements had to be just so in order that we could have enough resources to promote our growth and continued existence, even for the limited life span which we now enjoy. We had to have just enough protection from radiation through the atmosphere and the ozone layer. The celestial event which almost certainly exterminated the dinosaurs had to happen then and not a few million years later when it might have exterminated the mammals. Mankind had to lack the ability and perhaps the determination to exterminate each other before a sufficient degree of reason came into existence which persuaded them it might not be a terribly good idea to do so. Later on, when mutual extermination became much easier through the touch of a switch, there had to be just enough sanity in the Kremlin and the White House to prevent the rulers from doing so. Laying down the initial parameters, which led over a long period to this succession of chances and narrow margins, may seem like a rather hazardous intellectual pastime. It was clearly much more interesting to do it this way than simply to produce at one stroke the state of affairs which exists now or at any period of the past or future, without going through the interminable and complicated stages which have, in fact, led to our present situation. It may well be an open question whether we shall attain the state desired by the experimenter before we run out of time. If so, we may discover in a very long perspective of the future, what that purpose was. If not, we have to resign ourselves to being one of the failed experiments, to be succeeded by others, which, having learnt from what happened to us, may have a better chance of reaching the goal.

One of the riskiest elements in the sequence that has occurred up to now, from the point of view of the experimenter, was to endow us with a non-material element – spirit, soul etc. – which had two characteristics which may not necessarily have been part of the original intention. One is the propensity to think for ourselves, and to get outside the evolutionary process which seems to be laid down for us; that is to say to revolt against the course in which we find ourselves involved and seek to radically alter it. Secondly, this non-material element may possibly be able to survive the decay of the material universe and thus partake of the timelessness or infinite duration which, on our assumption, is enjoyed by the experimenter. On the other hand, it is possible that the competition may be welcomed with the thought that autonomous, timeless beings may add to the general store of existence and thus provide stepping stones to new areas of reality. It should have been anticipated – perhaps it *was* anticipated – that setting us the enormous puzzles which our science and philosophy try to deal with – the nature of matter, the nature of spirit (if any), the past and the future, the unravelling of purposes which led to these things being done, together with minds that were apparently endowed from the beginning with the desire to know the answers to puzzles – would have led to something like this in which the minds of such beings would be unwilling permanently to accept the role of intelligent machines and would aim for some more transcendental objectives. These puzzles would not have been present if man had been created at a single stroke at some given period of his existence such as the present, and therefore the value of the questioning of origins and purposes might not have been present. These speculations may possibly throw a little more light on the nature of our hypothetical experimenter, but they probably do not provide a completely satisfactory answer to this and many other questions. It will already have been apparent that the main object of the present enquiry is to ask unasked questions rather than to provide ready-made answers.

Chapter 10

Conclusion

The time has now come to sum up and to see whether we can set out intelligibly the elements of our situation which might seem to require, hopefully for the time being only, a myth to be invented, what these elements are and what kind of myth might best suit them, and provide some sort of temporary resting place for our speculations. We have dealt primarily with the question of origins, what happened before the Big Bang and who set it off; we have tried to grapple with the connection between timelessness and a time-bound system such as we live in; and also the question of the distant future after this universe will have come to and end, both as to whether we can foresee any means by which the human race – or something derived from it – can survive this point, and the further transition from a time-bound system back to timelessness, coupled with the difficulty of conceiving why our system should have been created out of a timeless situation if it is going to have a finite end, and what may be the alternative possibilities of extending our survival period.

We have looked at four possible ways in which the system we know might have originated. One is chance, which has the apparent advantage that it is not necessary to presume the existence of any being to start things going, or determine how they will go. But we came quickly to the thought that chance might not be quite as random as we might like to think in order to fulfil this requirement. In other words, do there not have to be rules by which chance operates, such as the rules of probability? If so, who lays down these rules? We do not get much help from considering the more ancient meanings of this concept. The nearest Greek equivalent was Tyche, who was made a daughter of Zeus in order to emphasise her importance in the scheme of things, but whose principal function seems to have been to decide which men should have good fortune and which should not. This is quite a long way from the concept of pure randomness, which is what we usually mean by chance nowadays. The word Tychism was coined in the late 19th century in English to describe a doctrine in which account must be taken of the element of chance in reasoning, and the explanation of the universe. This is coming very near to the subject of our enquiry. But it does not, at first sight, seem to mean the same as a doctrine that everything happens by chance and by no other reason. The Roman equivalent was Fortuna, but here again the primary meaning seems to have been the good or bad fortune that might be allotted to individuals. In order to fulfil our requirements, chance would have to operate in a continuum of particles or waves by bringing about an irregularity, which could lead to all subsequent cosmological developments, but this assumes that there is a continuum and merely sends us back to this other question of how did this originate. It could perhaps be argued that even this would be helpful in our search for the minimum act of origination, which we have set as our goal. All we would need would be the origination of a continuum, which means the absence of organisation of particles or whatever, and chance would then operate on this without any further outside intervention to produce the first collision or ripple from which all the rest could be derived.

One of the disadvantages is that we would be going on what has always seemed a remarkably absurd suggestion that if you set a group of monkeys before a group of typewriters and gave them infinite time to tap out whatever they wanted, they would sooner or later write the complete works of Shakespeare. This may be statistically correct, but to all common sense is an absurdity.

The second of our myths has been to think of one or more experimenters whose minimalist functions are to cause the Big Bang to take place and to lay down a series of rules by which the matter taking part in that event would combine, and the evolutionary system through which it would develop into the system that we know. Since we are talking of myths, it is, perhaps, not absolutely necessary to rule this out on the grounds that we then logically have to say who created the experimenters any more than the Greeks or other cosmological inventors had to say who invented the sky and the earth. For the same reason, the nature of the experimenter or experimenters would be difficult to define, except in a negative sense. They would be different from the God of, at any rate, the monotheistic religions, in several respects. One is that they would not be all-powerful. That is to say they do not, or could not, intervene in the process of the universe once they have got it going. They would not seek to impose a moralistic framework for it, but would be morally neutral and they could not be placated by prayer or sacrifice. The view taken in this enquiry is of this minimalist character, because the experimenters are only there because we cannot think of any other mechanism by which the Big Bang would have been initiated (other than the other hypotheses described in this section) and because giving them the attributes of God would, almost inevitably, lead to the creation of one or more religions, and therefore to the near certainty of exclusivity and conflicts. Having once come on the scene, men are left to get on with it and form their relations on a humanistic basis as described above.

A third possible origin for our existence would be that we are the product of a previously existing civilisation, which, seeing that its existence was threatened by one or other of the possible calamities we have described, set up an artificial intelligence which could continue its existence beyond the ending of the material circumstances in which the civilisation had existed, and programmed it to reproduce a civilisation similar to itself once a suitable site for this continued existence had been discovered. This alternative is, of course, not strictly speaking a hypothesis about origins, since it does not explain how the previous civilisation came into existence, for which we have to have recourse to one of the other myths. But it has some possible attractions so far as our own plight on this planet goes. It might also conceivably be brought to the aid of some of the unsolved problems of our own civilisation, such as the occasional jumps in the palaeological or archaeological records. It would perhaps be pushing things too far into the realms of fantasy to suppose that an artificial intelligence might be left over from a previous universe and be responsible for ours from the beginning, namely from the Big Bang onwards. It has to be remembered also that the possibility of an artificial intelligence, existing after the end of a material universe in which it was created, must remain speculative. This largely depends on whether it had discovered a means of keeping itself supplied with sufficient energy.

The next main candidate for the origination of our system is the supposition that a spirit world could have existed before our material world began, and could continue to exist after it. The existence of a spirit world is made known to us, so far as it may be believed that such a thing exists, by material means, that is to say by the evidence of our senses or our hallucinations. And the evidence, which we may feel able to put forward to justify such a belief, has to be recorded and communicated to others by material means. But we have argued that while the material world exists and is inhabited by people like us, it seems to be the case that spirits attach themselves to people, or are manifested to people with, however, the possibility that they have a separate existence which could be imagined to exist before and after the material world. One would then have to make the further leap of the imagination to suppose that it was this realm of the spirits which originated the material world, though for what purposes this might have been done must remain as obscure as most of the rest of this part of our discussion. The method by which spirits could interfere with matter, or impose their decisions on it, remains unknown, though a clue to the possible existence of the necessary power may be found in certain psychic operations such as the poltergeist phenomenon and in telekinesis. In both of these phenomena, material objects are visibly and materially affected by forces which cannot, at present, be detected by mechanical means or measured, and must therefore be regarded as being in a different kind of 'spiritual world'. There is of course a vast difference between such trivial psychic effects and the origination of the material universe. Nevertheless if the principle is accepted that such interaction is possible, we know of no reason at present to suppose that the same thing could not apply on a vastly greater scale. This hypothesis does not, of course, answer the question of who created the spirit world.

The final suggestion, which does not exactly provide an answer to the question of origins but changes considerably the picture which we are trying to describe and of which we are trying to find the origins, is to believe that there are numerous universes either taking place at the same time as ours or following in sequence. There are various forms, which this hypothesis can take. We have alluded above to one possibility, namely that owing to the operation of quantum mechanics it is possible that other universes are being created all the time by the indeterminacy of whether a wave is, or is not, observed at a certain moment, with the result that it can either lose its wave function and turn into particle at that point, or not, and the same thing happens later or not at all. Each solution appears to be equally valid scientifically, and it may be an accident which of them results in the kind of universe in which we perceive ourselves to be. Another version of the idea would be to suppose that this universe has been started by the experimenter, and that when it comes to an end, he may well press another button to start another experiment with a slightly or radically different universe. One of the features of almost any multiple universe theory is that it seems to be impossible to have communication from one universe to another. Of course the theory also gives rise to the question whether other universes are peopled by intelligences like ours and the further question of whether they are accompanied – as ours appears to be – by a non material element-spirit, which is capable of survival beyond the disappearance of the physical universe in which it happens to be temporarily located. This raises the curious picture of a survival state – heaven, if you like – peopled not only by dogs and dinosaurs but also by the spirits previously attached to little green men. There at last it may be hoped that communication across universes can be established.

The thought of multiple universes with potentially different lengths of survival and the thought of one universe preceding another by the whim of the experimenter goes some way towards bridging the gap which has proved so troublesome between timelessness and time-bound systems. There is no need to think that other universes have to come to an end so far as their physical status is concerned, like ours has to do. Indeed, it could perhaps be regarded as one of the failures of the current experiment that this is so, unless we accept the possibilities of prolonging a non-material existence such as we have described above.

All this is, of course, a great deal easier for those who believe in an eternal and all-powerful God. But this in itself also leads to problems that seem equally insoluble. For one thing, what could be the purpose of the creation of this world with all its complexities and its apparent extraordinarily wasteful use of resources other than as a textbook for mathematics and physics, or an essay in the application of moral philosophy. If such a being is thought of as being ultimately beneficent as well as all-powerful, then the insoluble question arises of the creation of evil or the contamination of the rest of creation by evil. We are also faced by the persistent question as to why the followers of an allegedly beneficent God should almost, without fail, form themselves into rival groups who persecute each other and persecute those who do not follow this God at all. This contradiction is powerful evidence against the simplistic view that we can account for the origins of the universe by assuming the existence of an all-powerful God, with beneficent motives in bringing about this creation. Otherwise one gets forced into the even more apparently contradictory belief that God created the world with its tendency to evil as well as good, in order that people would realise that they had to rely on themselves and not on the goodness handed down by one or other of the religions, allegedly based on the worship of this God. In other words, God created the world in the way he did in order to pave the way for the triumph of humanism. It is a curious result and it seems that you can get to the same position much more easily if you do not first have to go through the phases of belief in an all-powerful God, and the moral doctrines which he allegedly propagates. The object of the present enquiry has been to provide, for those who do not wish to go down this road, some choices of other means by which we are here, and also choices of the future, which may lie in store for us.